Liquid Thinking

Damian Hughes

CAPSTONE

Registered office
Capstone Publishing Ltd. (A Wiley Company), The Atrium, Southern
Gate, Chichester, West Sussex, PO19 8SQ, United Kingdom

For details of our global editorial offices, for customer services and for
information about how to apply for permission to reuse the copyright
material in this book please see our website at www.wiley.com.

978-1-90646542-1

A catalogue record for this book is available from the British Library.

Typeset in 9/10.5pt, Baskerville by Thomson Digital
Printed in the UK by TJ Interntaional, Padstow, Cornwall

Contents

Contents

Acknowledgements

This book wouldn't have been possible without the help of so many people. I'd like to offer my sincerest thanks to each of them and my apologies to anyone I have inadvertently missed out.

Geraldine, this book only exists because of your help, patience, advice, support and feedback. You don't know just how much you mean to me. Thanks for inspiring me.

Mum and Dad. Thanks for the encouragement, advice and constant inspiration. My heroes.

Chris, the best mate I could have.

Anthony and Rachael, thanks for the encouragement and web surfing.

Mari and Gerry, your attention to detail was phenomenal and your support vital. Thanks.

Chris Mallaband, the inventor of Liquid Thinking. Thanks, mate.

Phil Ince, the embodiment of Liquid Thinking. Thanks for being pernickety!

Iain and Andrea Allen, thanks for taking the time out from your own masterpiece to help.

Tracy Pettitt, thanks for the encouragement. Sorry for disturbing your train journeys!

Emma Finlay. The advice and unfailing support were amazing and invaluable. Remember me when you're running the place!

Dave and Vicky Morgan. Your guidance and advice kept this book on course when it looked like getting lost. Vicky, apologies for keeping him working late to read the many drafts.

Ben Jemison for helping set up www.liquidthinker.com
Nicky Wooton and Andrew Park from www.cognitivemedia .co.uk. Thanks for humouring me at Fouracres and backing the idea with your amazing support. Much appreciated.
Nobby Stiles, Sir Richard Branson, Angelo Dundee, Sir John Jones, Wayne Bennett and Chris Moon for offering your backing, support and encouragement.
Sue Schoormans for your support.
Chris Lunt. Thanks for your advice and guidance.
Brian and Christine Higginson. Inspirational.
Paul Lee. Respect.
Mark Holden. Good luck with the wedding.
Steve Byrne. What's next?
Gerry Fannon. Hope you and the boat make it to Ireland one day.
Andy Hardcastle. Please now say something nice about Human Racehorses.

Forza Malaka!
All Liquid Thinkers. Thanks for the inspiration.

About the author

Damian Hughes is the founder of the Liquid Company, which takes the methods used by great achievers and shows, in easy steps, how you can adopt them into your own life and business in order to achieve your dreams and ambitions. He is the author of *Liquid Leadership* and *The Survival Guide to Change*.

Hughes, a former England schoolboy footballer and Manchester United football coach, was a Human Resources Director for Unilever and led a turnaround in performance at the UK's oldest manufacturing site in Port Sunlight before carrying out similar work in Africa and the US.

He now runs his own change management consultancy, LiquidThinker Ltd, helping a wide range of individuals, teams and industries achieve similar employee engagement and success. He also works as a sports psychologist for the GB Rugby League team.

Hughes runs a Manchester inner-city youth club, Collyhurst and Moston, which has helped reduce crime and help many kids find a purpose in their lives, from stopping crime to winning Olympic medals. He was nominated for the 2007 William Hill Sports Book of the Year award for his biography of boxing great Sugar Ray Robinson.

His innovative and exciting approach has been praised by Sir Richard Branson, Muhammad Ali, Sir Terry Leahy, Tiger Woods, Jonny Wilkinson and Sir Alex Ferguson.

If you are interested in Damian working with you, contact him at damian@liquidthinker.com or visit his website at www.liquidthinker.com.

Foreword

Having read this book, I am flattered that I have been presented as a role model and am delighted to be asked by Damian to offer a foreword for *Liquid Thinking*.

As someone who has achieved many of my own personal goals and experienced the satisfaction from doing so, I would recommend that you adopt the lessons and techniques, which are captured in this excellent book, to greatly assist you in achieving your own ambitions.

Go ahead. Take the plunge and become a fellow liquid thinker.

Sir Richard Branson

Preface

Angelo Dundee is the best known of all boxing trainers. He is the most recognizable and famous and trained more than 20 world champions.

It gives me tremendous pleasure to be able to offer a contribution to this excellent book.

I have been involved with boxing for 60 years and have been fortunate enough to train and work closely with over 20 world champions, including some of the all-time greats like Muhammad Ali and Sugar Ray Leonard. It is for this reason that I feel able to comment on what makes the difference between the ordinary and the great, where the thin dividing line between success and failure lies and what separates the true champions from the contenders.

It is not purely talent. I have seen hundreds of talented fighters who have never achieved everything that they should have done. It is not down to luck. Luck can only carry you so far. It is not about how privileged your background is or where you come from. It is about your attitude, the mental approach which you choose to adopt to chase your dreams. Damian has done a remarkable job in capturing, in this book, the tips and techniques which the great people, like Muhammad Ali, knew about and used to perfection to be able to conquer the world.

Your ambitions may be more moderate than that, but it still shouldn't stop you using the same methods of the greats to help propel you towards your own goals.

Combine these with the determination to work hard and dedicate your whole self towards achieving whatever it is you desire and you, too, can become your own version of a world champion.

Good luck!

Angelo Dundee

Why read this book?

I have written *Liquid Thinking* for a number of reasons, but mainly because I have always wanted to write a book. So this is the fulfilment of one of my goals and I hope that you will give it some attention.

The second reason is that I am a genuine believer that we are all capable of more than we give. I therefore wanted to write a book that was a celebration of those we work alongside every day, as well as famous and well-known achievers – people who have given so much of themselves to achieve their own goals.

The final reason is that I wanted to find out what these people have in common, what characteristics they share and what lessons and advice they could give that would allow others to learn from them and go on to achieve their own special goals.

I want to offer two pieces of advice before you venture much further into this book:

1. Come along with an open mind. If I am right, think about what you have to gain. If you are determined to shoot down the lessons in the book and find fault, then I have no doubt that you will be successful. I also have no doubt that you will gain nothing from it. Don't close your mind to new possibilities.

2. Have a pencil with you when you read. This book is yours, so feel free to annotate or highlight any passages that strike a chord with you. There are actions for you to take at the end of each chapter – take time to work

on these. You may struggle with some of them at first. Don't worry, you can come back to them (skip to the chapter called "Perseverance" if you really need some convincing!), but do take the actions to get the absolute most out of this opportunity.

Creativity guru Edward de Bono suggested that 90 per cent of the mistakes we make in life are due to "solid thinking" – that is, an inability to see things from a different perspective. That is why this book is called *Liquid Thinking*. Applying its lessons to your life, goals and ambitions will open up a world of opportunities. Go on, have a go. What have you got to lose?

I look forward to hearing about your successes in applying the *Liquid Thinking* ideas and including them in the next volume.

CHAPTER 1

SINK OR SWIM

> " *No matter what your age, you are responsible for your own actions, irrespective of the actions or inactions of anybody else. If you are past the age of legal reason, you and only you are accountable for what you do or what you don't do.* "
>
> JERRY SPRINGER, TALK SHOW HOST AND FORMER MAYOR OF CINCINNATI

Jerry Springer, eh? And you thought this book would contain quotes from loads of famous dead people. Well, in my view his words are really relevant to this book and, more importantly, to you.

It is often said that there are three types of people in the world:

- those who make things happen

- those who watch what happened

- and those who say "What happened?"

I am continually amazed and fascinated by the number of people who either consciously or unconsciously believe in fate. What do I mean by that? Try it yourself – listen to your colleagues and your mates talking and count how many times a day you hear them say "if only". "If only the managers here knew how good I am . . . if only people would realise how talented I am . . . if only I had more money . . . if only I were a bit younger . . . if only I were older . . . if only I were in charge around here . . . if only people would listen to me . . . I'd be more successful."

Count how many times you hear yourself saying it (or words to that effect) – and then think about how much energy you're using up in moaning and what you could be using it for instead.

Woody Allen said that the world is run by the people who turn up. When you talk to any successful person, they all say that in life there are either results or excuses.

Or think about what writer George Bernard Shaw said:

" *People are always blaming circumstances for what they are. I don't believe in circumstances. The people who get on in this world are the people who get up and look for the circumstances that they want . . . and if they can't find them, they make them.* "

Richard Branson found the right circumstances to build a business. He decided to set up his Virgin Atlantic airline after he had tried to book a flight to New York and had spent a morning hitting the redial button on the phone, as the only current company doing flights to America was continually engaged. How many of us would find ourselves cursing and getting frustrated? Instead, he saw an opportunity. He reasoned that the company was either very poorly managed, in which case it would be an easy target for new competition, or so much in demand that there was room for new competition. He saw a result, not an excuse to give up trying.

Literally everything you do and everything you are – from how much money you earn to where you work, how successful you are as a parent, a friend or a workmate, and where you live – is a direct result of the decisions you have then made. You've made the decision to pick up this book and read up to this point. I would therefore encourage you to make another decision to read on. You'll read about the lessons you can learn from meeting and reading about successful people, and I hope the structure of the book will make you think and help you achieve what you really want.

Viktor Frankl was a Jewish prisoner who survived the Nazi concentration camps but saw his wife and children killed in them. He has written a book about his experiences and talks about how he was forced to face the worst possible circumstances anyone could imagine, but he still believed that he had a choice. The only thing the Nazis couldn't take from him was his own attitude. He made a deliberate decision that they would not dictate how he felt. He could choose that. He said:

" *We who lived in concentration camps can remember the men who walked through the huts comforting others, giving away their last piece of bread. They may have been few in number, but they offer sufficient proof that everything can be taken from a man but one thing: the last of the human freedoms – to choose one's attitude in any given set of circumstances, to choose one's own way.* "

If that powerful message isn't enough to persuade you to make a choice about your attitude, there is another good reason. You will live longer. You may respond to that by arguing that there is no way taking responsibility for yourself and your circumstances can influence your life expectancy, that lots of variables come into play: diet, work pressures, diseases and so on. So where could you do a study where everyone was submitted to the same environment? How about a convent?

A group of psychologists analysed the attitude of nuns before they entered a convent. They discovered that 90 per cent of the nuns who took personal responsibility for themselves and their lives were still alive at the age of 84. In contrast, only 34 per cent of those who didn't accept full accountability were alive.

Finally, if Jerry Springer is a little too lowbrow for you, I will finish off this chapter by quoting from another notable philosopher, Oprah Winfrey:

" *My philosophy is that not only are you responsible for your life, but you are responsible for doing your very best at it at this very moment, which will put you in the best place for the next moment.* "

Do you choose to sink or swim?

Action

Start to accept that you are 100 per cent accountable and responsible for you and your life, your feelings and every result you get. Stop making excuses and start to believe that you are the cause rather than the effect.

In 1964, when Russian leader Nikita Khrushchev was removed from power, he wrote two letters, which he handed to his successor, Brezhnev. He told him, when you get yourself into a situation that you are struggling to get out of, open the first letter. If it happens again, open the second one. Sure enough, trouble soon started to brew and eventually Brezhnev remembered the advice and opened up the first letter.

(Continued)

It read, "Blame everything on me." And so he told everyone that it was the fault of the old guy, Khrushchev, and the crisis died down and soon passed. Shortly afterwards, when another row threatened and trouble flared up again, Brezhnev remembered how effective the advice had been and so opened the second letter. This one said, "Start writing two letters."

Don't blame others. Accept personal responsibility.

CHAPTER 2

ARE YOU A DRIFTER?

" *We are each gifted in a unique and important way. It is our privilege and adventure to discover our own special light.* "

MARY DUNBAR

When you go to a funeral, do you ever find yourself thinking about your own funeral, how many people would come and who would be there? If you don't end up dismissing these thoughts as morbid or depressing, do you ever think about the funeral in a bit more detail and imagine what people would be saying about you? What do you think your family, your mates and your work colleagues would say about you? Stop for a second and consider this.

Beyond the usual comments about being great fun, always standing your round and being a good husband/wife/dad and so on, do you think anyone would be able to say what your purpose was, why you were on earth?

Wayne Bennett, a legendary Australian rugby league coach, summed this up well when, before a State of Origin match (*the* sporting series of Australia), he challenged his players to train and play as well as they possibly could, in order to fulfil the purpose which they had been assigned and which they were born to meet, with the words:

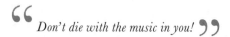 *Don't die with the music in you!*

What a brilliant phrase that is. What do you think is the music in you?

Psychologist Sigmund Freud called our purpose "the golden seed". At some stage in their formative years, most successful people remember someone telling them that they had a special talent. It could have been a teacher, a first boss, a priest, occasionally a relative, sometimes a mother or father. They tucked this private nugget away in their heart, but in times of doubt or uncertainty they pulled it out to reassure themselves that they were indeed pursuing their purpose.

Lance Armstrong, who fell in love with cycling at the age of 15, was influenced by his mother, who wanted him to keep fit and active. Richard Branson, one of Britain's most successful entrepreneurs, discovered his talent when he started a school magazine with some mates. Muhammad Ali's anger at feeling powerless to stop his bike being stolen by bigger, stronger kids led him to a boxing ring, where he was encouraged by his local police officer. For Tim Waterstone, the founder of the famous bookshops, it was a fascination with marketing along with his interest in books that fired his passion for bookselling. Thomas Edison, the inventor of the light bulb, was called a "stupid, muddle-headed blockhead" by a teacher at school. His mother who recognized his "golden seed" and she went to the school and told the teachers that her son possessed real intelligence. He said:

" *She cast over me an influence which has lasted all my life. The good effects of her early teachings and belief I can never lose. My mother never misunderstood or misjudged me.* "

We all have a unique purpose. So how do you discover yours?

Here are a few suggestions for you to think about:

Don't confuse your job and your purpose – they're not the same

Your job shouldn't define you. It should link in with your purpose, but it should not be your purpose. After all, what would you do if your job suddenly changed or disappeared? Think about how many people you know who have used the motivator of redundancy or retirement as a catalyst to go and do what they have always wanted. Your job should support what you have always wanted to do.

Richard Branson believes, "If you are working for what really matters – your purpose – you will give it all you've got."

Don't mistake your relationships for your purpose

Don't get me wrong. I'm not advocating that you leave your partner, but think of the film *Shirley Valentine*. She knew that her marriage didn't suit her life and so she fled to Greece to try and find her purpose. Your relationship should be consistent with your destiny, but it should not be your destiny. After all, a shared purpose is going to be even more powerful.

Your goals need to fit your purpose

I write about goals in a later chapter, but what you do on a day-to-day basis should fit with your purpose. Do you find that you easily get caught up in tackling problems for others rather than being able to devote time to yourself and your purpose? Success is not the result of luck or spontaneous combustion. You must first set yourself on fire. Are you too busy putting out fires to be able to start any of your own?

Your purpose doesn't have to be overly impressive

Your purpose doesn't have to be all about resolving world peace or curing cancer (you aren't a Miss World contestant), so don't feel a need to invent something that is. Your purpose has to impress only you.

Your purpose doesn't have to make you a martyr

Your purpose should fit you like a glove and should not be governed by what others think of it. You are going to be the person living your purpose and so if it excites you, that's all that counts.

Your purpose doesn't need to be complex

Keep your purpose simple. Let it say something that stirs your soul and helps you to realize you are here to achieve.

Jack Welch, the former head of General Electric who retired in 2001 after turning it into the world's most valuable company, said:

    Good business leaders also create a purpose, articulate this purpose, passionately own it and relentlessly drive it to completion.

Aim to have a clear purpose about what your life means and be able to explain what you are here to achieve.

A great example of someone who discovered their purpose is the seven-times Tour de France winner Lance Armstrong. At the age of 24 he was diagnosed with testicular cancer and doctors gave him only a 40 per cent chance of survival. He said:

    If children have the ability to ignore all odds and percentages, then maybe I – we all – can learn from them. When you think about it, what other choice is there than hope. In that situation, we all have two options, medically and emotionally: give up or fight like hell.

The evening before he was due to have brain surgery (the cancer had spread), Armstrong was forced to think about his own death, which was frighteningly real. He says that it was on this evening he recognized his own purpose in life:

    I believed in belief, for its own shining sake. We are so much stronger than we imagine and belief is one of the most valiant and long-lived human characteristics. To believe . . . that is a form of bravery. Without it, we would be left with nothing but an overwhelming doom, which will beat you.

His purpose wasn't to win cycling races – they were his goals – but by winning them, he proved that the power of belief can overcome the most difficult circumstances. After he had learned this he went on to win the gruelling Tour de France on a record seven consecutive occasions. When he first won it in 1999, he told the world's media:

" *When you get a second chance in life for something, believe in it and you will go all the way. I am proof of that.* "

What is your purpose?

Action

" *Here is Edward Bear coming downstairs now, bump, bump, bump on the back of his head, behind Christopher Robin. It is, as far as he knows, the only way of coming downstairs, but sometimes he feels that there really is another way, if only he could stop bumping for a moment and think of it.* "

A A Milne, *Winnie-the-Pooh*

This quote is a great example of our everyday lives. We have to move so fast just to get by that we never get the chance to stop and think about what we do and why we do it. Please take the time to stop and answer these questions, which will help you to identify what your purpose is:

What are the five things you love to do?

1.

2.

3.

(*Continued*)

4.

5.

What are the five things you are really good at?

1.

2.

3.

4.

5.

What do you consider is essential for you to do in life?

If you won the lottery, what are the three things you would do?

1.

2.

3.

If you were writing your own obituary to be read out at your funeral, what would you want it to say?

Now write down what your purpose is:

Liquid Thinkers

Andy Hardcastle

Imagine the scene. It's a crisp, cold winter's evening where you can see your breath forming in front of you in the clear, clean air as you sit at the wheel of your converted 1950 series 1 Land Rover in the middle of the beautiful Trentham countryside. You flex your fingers around the steering wheel to maintain your circulation and gently shake your head to ensure that the muscles in your neck and shoulders stay relaxed so that you can retain your focus and concentration. It's been a long drawn-out day since you woke this morning and competed in the first race at 8 a.m. You clear your mind of tiredness and fix your full focus on the section of the course that you are now required to tackle. You heard the muttered comments from the spectators about it being impossible and you make a deliberate effort to ignore them and block these negative thoughts out of your mind and instead turn them into positives. It isn't impossible. It's tough, sure, but you are in the final of the British Land Rover Championship. You don't expect it to be easy.

This is the second head-to-head challenge you have had to complete in the last few hours in order to be crowned as champion. The day had started out with 300 Land Rovers competing in the trial. The aim of the competition is to drive your vehicle over a difficult terrain, up steep hills, down fierce dips and through seemingly impossible angles as you weave through a course that is set up like a skiing slalom run. You lose points depending on how much contact you make with the wooden markers that mark the way. I had lost only 3 marks all day and now, after 12 sections and two individual duels, there was still no room to fit a cigarette paper between myself and Alex Skidmore.

The horn sounds to signal the start of my latest trial and although my neck, shoulders and body ache with the strain of pushing and pulling my 270 horsepower machine to its absolute maximum, my mind is fixed firmly on getting round with a perfect score. I manage it. I know I'm on fire and I know that I will not, I cannot, be beaten today.

When my rival again faces the same slalom and matches my achievements for the third time, I pull up alongside him. We look at each other and smile. "Nothing's going to separate us today, is it?" I ask. "What do you think about us sharing this title?" He doesn't say a word, just extends his hand and we shake. At that moment, I become the joint 2004 British champion – my finest and greatest achievement.

I've always been competitive in anything I do. I found the best outlet for my competitive nature at 16 when I started taking part in motorcycle trials. I progressed through the domestic ranks and eventually became regarded as a good club man at national level. I won a few 1st- and 2nd-class awards and even had a sponsor for a couple of seasons. I love the challenge of pitching your skills and abilities up against another person and then seeing who can come out on top. I despair these days when I hear about schools trying to remove competition from the classroom and preaching to the kids that there is no winning or losing. That's life, isn't it? It's not about getting beaten, it's all about what you take from a loss and learn from it, the positives you can glean from it. During the years I competed on motorbikes, this was my attitude and I loved the lessons it taught me in work and in life in general.

As I got into my late 40s, I noticed that I was starting to get more injuries and that it was taking me longer and longer to recover from them, which included a total of nine broken collarbones! I wanted to start looking at new horizons and new challenges. A friend suggested that we went down to a local Land Rover club show in Wales for a laugh and when I watched it, I started to think that this would be a perfect sport that I would be able to do in my dotage. I've also noticed that as men start to get older, they need bigger toys to play with. These huge beasts, which were being flung around the muddy, deeply rutted tracks with what looked like reckless abandon, looked big enough for me!

I bought myself a secondhand Land Rover 1955 Series 1 to be able to start competing. I entered my first competition in Wales with a massive amount of enthusiasm. I couldn't wait to get started.

I came last, by quite some distance.

My attitude to this was helped by the lessons I'd learned during my earlier career on two wheels. Rather than get despondent and beat myself up about it, I asked plenty of other people for their help and advice and they were only too happy to help. They suggested improvements I could make to the car and slowly I started to see my results improve.

A couple of years before I won the British Championship, I achieved another personal ambition at Trentham Gardens in 2002. I'd always said that I wanted to go through a whole trial course without losing any marks. It's a tough challenge and I'd gone close a couple of times, but I had noticed a pattern that after a lunch break, my concentration and focus dipped by 1 or 2 per cent and this tended to be when silly mistakes cropped up and points were lost. On that day I had a faultless morning and at lunchtime I kept myself apart from everyone else and monitored my thoughts, ensuring that only positive messages were in my mind, such as how well I was doing and how good a driver I was. When I returned behind the wheel I was feeling great and I flew through the first section without any errors. I knew I could do it.

On the very last section I was faced with a difficult uphill finish. I told myself that if I stuck to the same principles, I could do this. I measured the gaps and angles – using my Lever-issued tape measure! – and kept my Land Rover in a high gear with the clutch disengaged, my signature move. I flew up the hill and maintained my composure and concentration to the very last second and landed right between the finishing canes.

The stewards seemed to take an age to determine whether I'd scored a flawless round, but when they gave the signal to indicate that I had, I sounded my airhorn to signal my absolute joy. The other competitors heard this and understood. They joined in the chorus. At that minute, with the noise sounding like the Mersey on New

Year's Eve, I thought back to my first race when I trailed in last, and remembered my positive attitude and the lessons I had learned.

I have had some tough times in competition. One year I counted that I'd managed 18 complete revolutions as I turned the car over on numerous occasions. One time, after a particularly bad roll, I detached my retina and lost my sight for three days. That's why these days I wear a helmet and have earned myself the nickname Biggles.

I'd encourage anyone reading this book to try your best in whatever you do and enjoy it. I've seen fathers shouting at their kids during motorbike trials and it always strikes me that they are taking the fun out of the whole thing. You must enjoy what you do. That's what's important.

Don't aim to be perfect. Why not aim instead to be excellent? There are some courses where I know that I'm not going to get a clean score. Instead, I aim for the next best option. If I aimed for perfection, I might as well never bother to start.

Finally, set your sights high. Don't just aim to be the best in your locality. Look for the best person you know and measure yourself against them. If you are going to compete, you may as well try to be the best you possibly can.

CHAPTER 3

THIRST FOR SUCCESS

" *I dream, I test my dreams against my beliefs, I dare to take risks and I then execute my vision to make my dreams come true.* "

WALT DISNEY, FILM PRODUCER AND ANIMATOR (1901–66)

Did you know that in 1928 when Walt Disney was only 26 years old, he was on the train from New York back to Kansas when he drew a cartoon of a mouse on his sketchpad? Convinced that this drawing had the potential to be a success, he decided that he wanted to use it in a new form of film that had started to emerge called animation. In 1926, silent cartoons were still the only form of cartoon being produced, but Walt had the dream of his mouse featuring in the first cartoon with sound. In order to achieve this, he needed to raise approximately $15,000 to make the film. In today's money this would be about $1 million.

Now put yourself in the shoes of a New York bank manager and imagine that you are sitting at your desk opposite a 26-year-old lad who is asking you for a $1 million loan in order to make a new type of film, which doesn't even exist yet, but it involves a mouse. He has no real track record of success and has no savings of his own that he can use to offset the risk. What would you say? Think about it.

Like you probably would, Walt's bank manager laughed him out of the bank.

Undeterred, Walt popped along to another bank to present his plan and request the money. He received a similar reaction to his first visit and so he went to another, and another, and another, and . . . Are you starting to get the idea?

Imagine yourself in the same situation as Walt Disney. How many banks do you think that you would have visited, receiving a mixture of negative, hostile and bemused reactions, before you gave up and thought of something better to do? One? Two? Ten? Twenty?

Walt Disney visited 305 banks before he found one that was prepared to take a gamble on him. He had a thirst for success and knew what he wanted to achieve; and he was prepared to pursue it relentlessly, whatever the cost.

Numerous studies have proved that successful people have a really clear and defined vision of what they want to do with their lives. They possess a crystal-clear goal that lets them chase their passion rather than chase their pension. In the last chapter I encouraged you to think about what you want out of life and what you need to achieve to fulfil your purpose.

Now let's examine what it means to be successful. Winston Churchill thought that success was about being able to go from "one disaster to another without any loss of enthusiasm" until we achieve what we want (305 banks, remember!).

Success is different for all of us, but below are some basic definitions.

Success is a journey, not a destination

When Jack Dempsey retired as undefeated world heavy-weight champion, he was asked what it had felt like to achieve his ambition. Dempsey had grown up as a home-less kid and had become champion during the Great Depression of the 1920s. He viewed his purpose as being someone who gave hope to others. He said:

    ❝ *Becoming heavyweight champion of the world was the culmination of a dream but I loved the whole journey I made along the way.* ❞

It should be a pleasure to pursue your purpose, not a chore or a task, and it shouldn't be just about you getting to a particular place. You should enjoy the *process* of getting there.

This reminds me of a great speech by Edward B Nervill, vice-president of General Motors, just before he retired:

66 *Let us recognize a basic truth. Success in life is not a destination. It is a journey. Fortunately, this means that no one is obliged to work towards a single, distant goal and be judged successful only if he attains that one objective. As with a traveller, the end of the journey is usually beyond the range of vision, but there is much of interest and beauty along the way to reward each day's steps. The happiest journey is not made with downcast eyes which see only tired, dusty feet. It is made with uplifted sight to appreciate its significance and to picture what may be beyond. The stars were made for those who look up and whose imagination knows no limits.*

When I am feeling sorry for myself, I simply go for a walk and I keep on walking and walking, looking around me as I go – at the front doors that hide other people's fears and joys, at the marvels of nature, at the courage and invention behind every church and factory, at the sheer size and complexity of the small part of the world my legs can cover. And if that doesn't make my worries seem insignificant by comparison, I get rat-arsed! 99

Success is the realization of your dream

The more you focus and think about your purpose on the inside, the more it materializes on the outside. In other words, if it can exist in your head and heart, you should be able to hold it in your hands and know when you have attained it.

Imagine being Walt Disney on 19 November 1928 holding a copy of the *New York Times*, containing a review of *Steamboat Willie*, the first speaking cartoon, which premiered the previous evening and which the paper described as "ingenious and a good deal of fun". That idea had been in your head two years earlier on the train journey when you first drew Mortimer Mouse (who later became Mickey) and now you can hold its success in your hands. That's the realization of a dream.

Success is a worthy goal

What you define as success should be a goal that you are in love with and enjoy chasing. Don't ask if you are capable or worthy of it, but ask whether it is a goal that is worthy of you and your efforts.

When speaking about her work to set up a home to care for street children, Mother Teresa of Calcutta explained, "The success of love is in the loving – it is not in the result of loving."

A young Sven-Göran Eriksson regularly visited England when he started coaching in Sweden and he studied the training methods of the leading football coaches of the day, spending some time with Bob Paisley, the legendary Liverpool manager. He vividly remembers seeing Paisley dancing around on the touchline after a Liverpool goal:

> " *In that moment, I had a glimpse of what makes him tick. Here was a man so passionate and in love with the game and obsessed with winning.* "

Paisley agreed:

> " *I hear and read about what makes a successful manager but it is the same for anyone who is successful. The basic factor is enjoyment. It is vital to have that.* "

Success is a choice, a decision: what do you want to be, to do and to have?

This is my favourite definition of success and is summed up by a quote from singer/songwriter Joan Baez:

> " *You don't get to choose how you're going to die. Or when. You can only decide how you are going to live. Now!* "

Kenyan long-distance athlete Kip Keino once approached his American coach, Lou Tice, and they discussed their preparations for the upcoming 10,000-metre race at the World Championships.

They discussed race tactics and the coach suggested that when Keino heard the bell to signal the 25th and final lap, he should attack hard and run this lap faster than any of the previous 24. Keino didn't agree and explained that it was at this stage when his lungs burnt and his legs felt sore and his heart raced furiously. He saw this request from his coach as impossible. Tice stopped and thought.

Eventually he asked Keino why he chose to run and compete. Keino explained the great pride he felt knowing that the whole continent of Africa, along with his country, his village and his family, would be watching him compete on the highest stage of all.

Tice listened intently and then said that he had thought about it and revised his tactics. He told Keino that when he heard the bell for the final lap, he should sit on the kerb; if he did this for a few seconds, his lungs, legs and heart would soon feel a lot better and then he could continue to run.

Keino blinked in disbelief at this advice and said, "But if I do that, I won't win the race!"

The coach nodded and replied, "Exactly. You can choose to run and you can choose whether you are going to give your best or not."

An American sociologist, Dr Anthony Campolo, did some research in which a group of elderly people, all aged 95 or over, were asked the following question: "If you were to live your life over again, what would you do differently next time?"

According to Campolo, the top three answers could be summarized as follows:

- *Have fewer regrets.* This related more to what people didn't do than what they did do in their lives.

- *Take more time out to reflect.* Some people felt that they just drifted along with the crowd and spent little, if any, time considering what they really wanted from life. Think about this. If you've read up to this point in the book and thought about the questions it asks, you aren't one of those people, are you? You've taken the time to reflect and you should congratulate yourself.

- *Leave a legacy*. People wanted to feel that their lives had counted for something and that in some way they would be remembered after they had gone. In other words, they wanted the people at their funeral to know what their purpose was, what they stood for.

Most people will go to the time and effort of writing a will at some stage to say what they want to happen after they die. Fewer people put the same effort and attention into what they want to happen while they are alive. You have the chance to start now.

Sir John Jones, the headmaster of the UK's worst school who transformed it into the most improved school in seven years, said that 85 per cent of us will go to the grave having only used a maximum of 15 per cent of our potential.

You have a choice whether you want to remain among that 85 per cent.

Action

Think about what is most important to you and what you most enjoy doing. What makes you happy? Ask the people you care about what success means to them. The more time you spend thinking about what success means to you, the more likely success is to happen.

Consider what success means to you in relation to your career (paid or unpaid work), your relationships and your recreation time.

Write down what success would look, feel and sound like for you, both now and in five years' time.

Some questions to help you answer this are:

- Write a list of things that you don't like doing. Make the list as long as you like.

- Write a list of things that you do like doing. Make the list as long as you like.

- When does time seem to fly? What do you do, at work or at play, that makes time pass quickly? Write a list of those things. Make the list as long as you like.

- Think about what energizes you. Which things make you feel better after you've completed them than you did before you started? Make a list of all those things. Make it as long as you like.

(Continued)

- Think about the things you are good at. Include things you do at work and at play. Write a list of everything you are good at. Make it as long as you like.

- Now look at the list of things you are good at and cross out any that you may do well, but that don't energize you, that you leave to the end of the day or that make time drag.

Now you should have a clearer idea of what you may want to include in your life to help you become a success.

CHAPTER 4

LIQUID GO(a)LD

"*If you are going to be having goals, you might as well make them big ones!*"

DONALD TRUMP, BUSINESS MAGNATE AND TELEVISION PERSONALITY

In the 1950s, a study carried out at Harvard University asked students whether they had goals. Not surprisingly, virtually everyone said that they did. They were then asked how many had actually put these goals down in writing and the answer to this question was only 3 per cent of the group.

This study was followed up 30 years later and the 3 per cent who had written down their goals were worth more than the other 97 per cent combined.

Amazing or just a coincidence?

That's up to you to decide, but as long as your goals only stay inside your head, you run the risk of them only ever being dreams. Remember, I highlighted in the last chapter that success is a choice you can make. You can't necessarily have everything you want, but you can have anything you want. The choice you face is what you want to be, to do and to have. You have to make some decisions about how you are going to spend your time and where you are going to put your energies, otherwise one day you'll wake up at 100 years old and be answering questions about your biggest regrets in life.

When you think about your goals, ask yourself whether you're a hen or a pig. When it comes to ham and eggs, the hen is merely involved but the pig is committed.

SMART RAS

This isn't a spelling mistake. Let me explain.

Having a written goal is more likely to get you into the top 3 per cent of the wealth population. If you are going to go to the trouble of writing down a goal, I would suggest that you copy the example of many successful people, such as the golfer Greg Norman:

66 *Setting goals for your game is an art. The trick is in setting them at the right level, neither too low nor too high.* 99

Imagine you have a goal to lose some weight. That's pretty vague, isn't it? Instead, use the SMARTS method and make your goals:

- *Specific*. Define exactly what you want to accomplish and focus on only one thing.

  Example: "I want to lose two stone in weight by March 2010."

- *Measurable*. Use percentages, cost, quality, numbers – it doesn't matter what, but you should think of all of the ways you can measure your progress in order to be able to say whether you did or didn't achieve it.

  Example: Giving a clear measure of weight you want to lose (two stone) and a time measure (by March 2010) makes your goal measurable.

- *Achievable and Realistic*. Think of something that is within reach but still requires you stretch to achieve it.

  Example: Is two stone a realistic amount of weight to lose or are you kidding yourself?

  This is your decision, as what may be achievable and realistic for you may not be for someone else. For example, your goal might be to run the London Marathon in 4 hours. For Paula Radcliffe that would be a gentle jog.

If that voice in your head is telling you as you write your goal that you won't do it, the likelihood is that you won't. When you write the goal, write it as though you have already achieved it, in the present tense, and use your senses to describe it. For example:

"I feel and look great now that I have lost weight."

Why should you do this? Well, every time you read your goal (put it somewhere you'll see it every day, like by your bed or on the fridge) your unconscious mind, your emotions and your RAS (more of that later) will kick in and support you in getting there.

- *Timed.* Set yourself a deadline by which you will achieve your goal. Be careful not to limit yourself by setting a goal that is too far in the future. At the same time, a goal that it is too close can cause you to become demotivated instead, so it's a question of finding the right balance.

  Example: March 2010. Is six months a realistic timescale? It's not too far in the future that you can't imagine it, yet it's not too near to be unrealistic.

- *Step.* The last step. What hard evidence will you need to prove to yourself that you have fulfilled your goal, that you have done it? If your goal is about buying a house, it might be the moment you put the key in the lock or the minute you see the SOLD sign being taken down.

  Karen Darke, who was paralysed at 21 after a climbing accident and who then achieved her dream of cycling across the Himalayas, explained that her step was the moment she watched the sun setting from the top of a mountain she'd spent the previous couple of hours cycling up. Mark Holden, a Liquid Thinker who tells his story later in this book, described his step as imagining himself enjoying a beer with his fiancée after completing the London Marathon.

If you don't make the effort to write down what you will see, hear, smell, touch and feel at the moment of your step, you may fall short before you achieve your goal.

Example: Imagine yourself standing in front of a full-length mirror in your bedroom trying on a new pair of jeans that you really wanted to be able to wear.

66 *Many of life's failures are people who did not realize how close they were to success when they gave up.* 99

This was said by Thomas Edison, the inventor who as we've seen was described by his teachers as a "blockhead", who carried out over 10,000 experiments, using over 3000 different types of material, including coconut hair, fishing line and bamboo, before he found success with the light bulb and was able to light the world! Do you think that his step was seeing a light bulb above his head?

Let's talk about your RAS. I'm not being rude here.

You will find that if you do take the time to think about and write down what your SMART goal is, 80 per cent of how you achieve it will take care of itself. Bear with me while I explain why writing down your SMART goal will ensure that "a whole stream of events . . . unforeseen incidents and meetings . . . which no man could have dreamt will come your way", as German writer and scientist Goethe put it.

This is down to your RAS, which stands for Reticular Activating System (RAS), a small part of your brain that is critical in helping you achieve your goals.

When you drive to work, how often do you notice the small details of your journey? Do you notice if they have painted the door of No. 29 green instead of red? Do you notice that the daffodils outside No. 10 are now in bloom? Do you spot that the curtains in No. 45 are blue? I thought not. This is because your brain is receiving about two million pieces of data a second. If you were able to process all of this information, your brain would, quite literally, explode. And so you are only conscious of a few pieces of information at any one time.

OK, so imagine you're driving through Tesco's car park, looking for a space. Suddenly you start to become aware of people carrying shopping bags and walking slowly, reverse lights on cars coming on and all sorts of other details that you would normally miss because you now need a parking space. This is your RAS working for you.

Stop for a second and think about your left foot and whether it is comfortable inside your shoe. Where was that thought until I just brought it to your attention? The answer is nowhere. You were looking after it on an unconscious level until I kicked your RAS into action.

Here's one last example of your RAS. Have you ever had a goal to own a particular type of car, let's say a yellow VW Beetle? Once you have decided what car you want, have you ever noticed how you suddenly start to see loads of that car on the road, whereas before you hadn't?

It is not that these cars weren't previously there, it's just that you weren't conscious of them before.

It's the same when you set yourself a goal that you really want. Suddenly you will find all sorts of coincidences and opportunities coming your way, which will help and support you in achieving your goal. Once I had decided that I wanted to write this book, I started to find ideas and quotes to use in it everywhere I looked, in the newspapers, on television and in conversations. One of the quotes I found was from former US President Abraham Lincoln, and I think it neatly wraps up this chapter:

" *When you know what you want to achieve, what your goal is, you will start to find yourself unconsciously keeping away from people and circumstances which continually knock what you are trying to achieve. It is small people who do that. You will also, unconsciously seek out and find yourself in the company of great people, who will support you and help you to recognize opportunities where there were previously none.* "

See, it does pay to be a SMART RAS.

Action

There are two basic parts to goal setting, which include taking small steps and then writing your goals in the SMARTS format. It will be most

(Continued)

37

useful for you to start thinking about small steps and then move on to writing them SMARTS.

Small steps

The most useful and easy way to start setting your goals is to get rid of your "shoulds" (things you feel you should be doing but for whatever reason you aren't).

- Step 1: Define all your shoulds". Example: I should lose some weight.

- Step 2: Explore reasons for your shoulds. Example: Because I don't feel confident about myself. Because it isn't healthy to be overweight, etc.

- Step 3: Change "should" to "want to". Example: I want to lose some weight.

- Step 4: Make your want positive. Example: I want to be slimmer!

SMARTS

Now make your want SMARTS:

- Specific

- Measurable

- Achievable

- Realistic

- Timed

- Step

Example: It is March 2009 and I have lost two stone in weight and I now weigh 12 stone. I am standing in front of the mirror in my bedroom wearing a new shirt and jeans and I feel fitter, healthier and great.

Now, follow these steps and write your goal below:

Liquid Thinkers

Mark Holden

I am the manager of a local Sunday football team, which is something I've done for the last few years, ever since I injured my knee. One week, one of the lads from the team had been talking in the dressing room about his plans to run the London Marathon and it started to get me thinking.

Running a marathon, especially the London Marathon, was one of those things that had always been bubbling away in the back of my mind, something I'd get round to doing, one day. I'd never thought about it in any specific terms. It had always seemed like a difficult but achievable challenge and so I decided to give my old manager a call, as I knew that he had run it a couple of times before. At this stage I only wanted to know a little bit more about it, but once we started chatting and he told me how fantastic the feeling of actually taking part and finishing it was, I knew there and then that I would do it.

If you had stopped me and asked me what sort of picture I had in my mind when I thought about the marathon, it was probably the sort of image you see on the telly: the finishing line, next to Buckingham Palace, loads of people cheering and going mad, that sort of thing. I imagined myself running at full speed through the line. I suppose it was this sort of picture in my head that got me feeling excited about doing it. I hadn't given any thought at this stage to the hard work that would be involved.

I have got a bit of a reputation among my mates and my family of being a "fly-by-night" sort of person. You know, the sort of fella who loses interest in things really quickly. Let me give you an example. When I moved into our new house, over a year ago, I did just enough work to get comfy in it and I've been managing to put off doing the other jobs that need doing. I'm not lazy; it's because the house is just comfortable enough.

So when I told my girlfriend what I was planning to do, she didn't really think I was serious at first. We enjoy a good social life and we like going out quite a lot, so she thought there was no way I wanted to do the marathon enough to cut down on the socializing and give the training my full commitment.

This time, I knew differently. I started from the fact that I knew I was going to finish the marathon, one way or another, then I worked backwards from there. I started to think about how I could plan my training and preparation. I knew that I needed to cut down on the ale and start eating better, as this would help my energy levels. I decided I could make better use of my days off and so I set myself some small targets, such as "If I cut the lawn in the morning, I will play golf in the afternoon", that sort of thing. Being able to set goals like this made it easier for me to plan and to make time to get out and train.

I did involve others and had a training partner, a mate from work who was also running the marathon, but most of the time I went out on my own. My routine was to do a day on and a day off and gradually I built up, so that I was running between 8 and 15 miles along the Wirral peninsula pretty regularly.

I really started to enjoy the feeling of being able to run farther than I thought I could and I liked the fact that I could feel myself improving and getting better the more I did it. I won't lie, I'll admit that there were some days when the weather was terrible and I just didn't fancy going out and running, but I tempted myself with that image of me crossing the finish line in London and imagined the feeling of achievement I knew I would enjoy when I did complete it, and this made me go out. I would have felt a bigger failure if I'd pulled out before even attempting it than if I had somehow failed to finish on the day.

In the days and weeks beforehand, I spoke to loads of people I knew had completed a marathon and I wasn't afraid to ask questions about how they had prepared and how it felt to succeed. This was a big help: knowing that plenty of other people had been there and done it gave me a confidence boost and everyone was really encouraging. They were all happy to share little tips and bits of advice.

The day itself was boiling hot and there wasn't a lot of wind about, which made it feel even more humid. Not ideal conditions to run 26.1 miles in. The atmosphere was amazing, though, and I was surprised how much this really helped to keep me going. Little kids would hold out their hands for me to "high five" as I ran past and people came out of the pubs along the route to cheer and shout encouragement. By the end of the first half of the race I was feeling good.

People had warned me about the stage all runners face, when you start to hurt and when doubts flood into your mind. I "hit the wall" at 14 miles. This was the time I really did start to doubt whether I could carry on.

I knew, though, that it was a mental battle and I started to tell myself that I had run this distance in training loads of times before and that every pace I took was a pace closer to finishing. What helped was when I pictured myself running 5 miles in training and this allowed me to keep telling myself that I could do it. The crowd were also a massive help as they continued to shout encouragement. Slowly and gradually, I started to feel better and managed to keep going.

The feeling I experienced when I did run past Buckingham Palace and crossed the finishing line was absolutely amazing and was even better than I'd imagined it would be when I'd first pictured that very same image in my mind.

I had started out with a target of running the marathon in around 4 hours and even though I came in just outside this time, the sense of elation and satisfaction was overwhelming.

Would I do it again? Definitely. I am currently trying to persuade my fiancée that it's a good idea, as we get married five days after next year's marathon!

CHAPTER 5

WHAT ARE YOUR ANCHORS?

" *The biggest problem with most people of today is that they don't stand for anything. Values provide directions. If you don't stand for something, you fall for everything.* "

DON SHULA, HEAD COACH OF MIAMI DOLPHINS

What are your anchors? By that I mean the values, the mood, the emotions and the states you most enjoy being in. What does it take to make you happy?

I have met a number of people who have gone through a health scare and afterwards have found peace within themselves. I have asked them what difference the event made to them and some of them have explained that it took the scare of nearly losing everything to make them realize just what was important to them.

Now, without putting yourself through a near-death experience, take the time to stop and think about what is really valuable to you and your ongoing happiness.

Once you know your values, you can construct your life's purpose and goals around them to ensure that when you reach your chosen destination and achieve your goals, you have done it in a way that will leave you feeling satisfied. Take the Canadian sprinter Ben Johnson. If his values were about truth and honesty, do you think that when he won the 100m gold medal in Seoul in 1988 he would have felt great, knowing that he had done it through the illegal use of steroids?

A great example of someone who met their goals without having to compromise their values was Muhammad Ali. In 1967, during his first reign as world heavyweight champion, he was drafted into the US Army and ordered to go to Vietnam to fight. Despite the government's threats to strip him of the world title, which he coveted and had worked so hard to achieve, and the possibility of being thrown into prison for his refusal to be drafted, Ali knew his values, which included the belief that the war was wrong. He would not let himself be compromised, even when he was given the offer of being a figurehead for the army and of never having to face any conflict. He famously declared, "I ain't got no quarrel with the Vietcong."

Instead, Ali accepted that he had to lose his title and wasn't able to fight again for over three years because his purpose, which was "to be the greatest", and his goal, which was to be the heavyweight champion of the world, would have felt hollow and worthless had he sacrificed his own values to achieve them.

Values are the rules around which we construct our lives. Nobody else can make you have particular values: they are unique to you and you alone, as they are the rules by which you choose to live and around which you chase your version of success.

Think about your own values and how many of them are rules that are realistic, and how many rules by which you can never hope to win.

Let me give you an example. How many of you think that you would be really, truly happy and all your worries would be over if you came into a lot of money, like winning the lottery? I am sure you are aware that the odds on actually winning the lottery are about 14 million to one (my favourite way of explaining it is that you are more likely to go up to a stranger in a foreign country and guess their telephone number than win the lottery!). So why would you have this as a rule for making yourself truly happy? Wouldn't it be better to follow the examples of those who have had health scares and tell us that they set rules for achieving happiness, such as being genuinely grateful to wake up in the morning, which are achievable for everyone?

Here's an idea of different things you might consider to be a value:

- **Success:** do you want to be successful? Do you want to be the best in your chosen field?

- **Passion:** is that something you are excited about? Do you want to experience huge passion in everything you do and so will go the extra mile and do whatever it takes to feel it?

- **Fun:** do you have fun as one of your values? Do you want to enjoy life to the full?

- **Greed:** It was Michael Douglas's character, Gordon Gecko, in the film *Wall Street* who said "greed is good", but you could choose this as one of your values if you are the sort of person who just wants more, more, more.

- **Enthusiasm:** are you the kind of person who leaps out of bed determined to squeeze the most out of the day?

- **Power:** is power important to you? Do you want people to look at you and see someone who brings power to a situation?

- **Love:** to love other people and to be loved. How do you feel about love?

- **Integrity/honesty:** do you believe that truth is high on your list of values? Do you believe in telling the truth even if the consequences may be unfortunate?

- **Recognition:** you may wonder how you could have recognition as a value, but some people do, because it plays an important part in their lives.

- **Control:** is this a value for you? Do you want to be in control? Do you want to know exactly what's happening every minute of the day? Is control important to you and are you really clear about where you want to go? Are you a hands-on type of person?

- **Blame:** do you find yourself blaming others for situations that occur around you? Do you want to know who is causing the problems so that you can get to the bottom of them?

- **Excitement:** are you the type of person who loves bungee-jumping, jumping off cliffs or taking risks? Do you think that excitement is within the business and the work you do? Do you think that excitement is found within relationships? Could it be one of your values?

- **Security:** do you want to be secure? Do you want to know exactly where everything is going to be on a regular basis? Do you get home and love to know that certain things are going to be in a certain place? Do you like the feeling of total security?

- **Worry:** do you find yourself worrying all the time? Do you believe that worrying is a way of showing that you care?

- **Contribution:** do you believe that making a contribution is critical? Do you want to give your time and efforts to helping others without any recognition? Are you the sort of person who is always the first volunteer?

- **Health:** are you focused on your health? Do you carefully watch what you eat, believing that nourishment and vitality are the keys to quality of life?

- **Creativity:** do you aim to be creative in all you do? Are you continually trying to think of new ways to do things? Do you think it's important to think outside the box and move the boundaries?

Even Homer Simpson knows what his values are:

" *There is an empty spot I've always had inside me. I tried to fill it with family, religion, community service but those were dead ends. I think that this chair and a beer is the answer.* "

Action

1. Consider the values that your parents, mentors and teachers held. Write a list of them.

    Take a look at the values you wrote down above and consider which you feel you should share, and those you actually do share.

2. Think about the times when you truly felt successful, when you surprised yourself how well you did. Write a list of these times.

    Now take a look at the list above. Can you think of a value, something you believe in, that helped inspire that success? For example, maybe you won a running race against all odds. The value that led you may have been practice or self-belief or hard work or education or teamwork.

---

3. Go back to the chapter where you wrote about what success means to you. Do you begin to see your values emerging?

What are the five most important values in your life and work? What are the rules and conditions that will allow you to live your life and make decisions that suit your personal rule book?

1.

2.

3.

4.

5.

CHAPTER 6
FUTURE REFLECTIONS

" *The man who has no imagination, has no wings.* "

MUHAMMAD ALI, THREE-TIME WORLD HEAVYWEIGHT
CHAMPION BOXER

Let's return to the example of Muhammad Ali, the most famous sportsman in history. It was Ali who coined the phrase "future history" and he offers the best example of what that means. When he burst onto the world boxing scene, he was the first sportsman to make bold predictions about which round he was going to win in. He would confidently declare his chosen route of victory in poetry, such as:

> *This boy likes to mix, so he'll fall in 6!*

He went on to make this sort of prediction in 19 of his 61 fights. How many times do you think he was accurate with his prediction of the round he would win in?

The actual answer is 17.

In 1963, before he became heavyweight champion, Ali fought Archie Moore, a well-respected former champion. Many people viewed this as the first real test of his career. At the press conference, Ali looked at the huge, imposing giant he was going to face and said:

> *Don't block the aisles, don't block the door. You will all go home, when Archie goes in four!*

Archie Moore, a man with many years of ring craft and experience, couldn't believe the audacity of this cocky kid. He thought Ali was crazy and just laughed.

After the press conference, Ali went back to his hotel room, lay down and relaxed from his head to his toes and he began to use his imagination.

In his mind, he saw the press conference just as it had been. He saw himself making that prediction, but then he started to visualize the days and weeks ahead and saw himself building up to the fight. He saw himself doing amazing things in training: imagining himself preparing and getting stronger and better than Moore. He knew that if Moore was up at 5.00 a.m. to do his road work, he'd be up at 4.00 a.m. Ali envisioned himself during his sparring sessions, getting bigger and stronger.

He then imagined the day of the fight and himself arriving outside the stadium and getting out of the car, hearing the crowd chant only one name. He could hear it over and over again: "Ali, Ali . . . " He would intensify the image, increase the feeling, bringing it closer to him, imagining and feeling every single word, every single emotion that went with it.

Then he pictured himself going into the dressing room and imagined the feeling of the bandages being wrapped on his hands, feeling the gloves being laced on and he saw himself standing strong. He heard the announcement of his name as he walked into the arena. In his own mind, he sensed the crowd going crazy, screaming for him. They were screaming only his name; everybody was on his side.

In his vision, he saw himself getting into the ring and looking across the crowd. He could see every single person screaming his name and he could hear it over and over again, intensifying, increasing in volume, increasing in emotion: "Ali, Ali . . . " Then he turned to face Moore and saw him shrink small. They touched gloves and started to fight.

Ali saw the first three rounds in perfect focus, mentally rehearsing the outcome he wanted. He saw everything exactly as he had planned it. Connecting, brilliant blows, doing the famous Ali shuffle, floating like a butterfly, stinging like a bee!

And then, as the bell signalled the start of the fourth round, he moved out purposefully into the ring's centre. He waited patiently until the right moment. Boom! He connected with Moore and saw him go down. When he fell, Ali imagined himself standing over Moore and the referee making the count – "one, two, three . . . ". At the point he knew he had won, he would freeze-frame the image and surround it in brilliant white light. This image was his "future history".

By the way, he did go on to win in the 4th round.

How about this as a further example of the power of future history? At the University of California, Los Angeles in California, the coach divided his basketball team into three groups. He got every player to throw 100 shots and then calculated how many each group had scored in total. He gave the groups different sorts of practice. One group did nothing; the next group stayed on court and practised shooting hoops, where the players take a free throw at the basket; and the third group went back to the dressing room and were made to sit quietly and just picture themselves shooting hoops and imagining how the ball would feel in their hands, the sound of the ball rattling through the basket and the emotions they would feel when it went through. The three groups did the same activity for a month. The coach brought all of the groups back onto court and had a competition to see which one would score the most consecutive points. Guess who won? You've got it. The team who had done the visualization exercise. To check that the result wasn't a fluke, the coach tried it for a further month and guess what? The group who had continued the mental rehearsal won even by an even higher score.

Still need convincing?

How about this one then? Psychologists in the UK have devised a mental training system that can increase your golf putting skills by 50 per cent in six weeks. A group of amateur golfers were given a choice of either watching a video of themselves or listening to an audio tape of their putts being holed for 10 minutes a day. They were not allowed to go onto a course and physically practise any putts; they could re-create the movement in their heads only. At the end of six weeks, both groups had improved massively. The group using video increased their putting skills by 57 per cent and the group using audio tapes increased by 47 per cent. No one had actually picked up a club during that period! The result was purely down to the power of the mind being able to conjure up images of success.

Convinced yet? Well, you should be, as if you use the same simple techniques and methods of clearly picturing and visualizing what you want, your chances of success start to improve dramatically.

Action

Here is a brilliant exercise that is worth trying with a friend or your partner. Find a quiet place and ask your partner to sit and listen to you. It isn't a
(*Continued*)

conversation as you will be doing most of the talking. Imagine that it is two years ahead in time and you are looking back at those two years. Answer the following questions (remember to use the past tense, such as "I have" or "I did"):

1. Where have you been on holiday? Was it good? What did you do? Who did you go with?

2. Where are you living? Describe your house. Who are you living with? (Take care in answering this question if you are with a partner!)

3. Where are you working? What has work been like? Are you still doing the same job?

4. What have you achieved in the last couple of years that you are most proud of and why?

Generally, when you talk about what you are going to do, it tends to be at some unspecified point in the future ("one day I'm going to . . . ") and it tends to focus on the action itself (" . . . I'll paint the fence!"). In contrast, when you look at your "future history", the exercise is all about you have done and, most significantly, it engages your emotions, as it focuses on what you have already achieved. If you can't get excited about your achievements, who will?

When you did the future thinking exercise, did you quickly find yourself running out of things to say? That isn't a problem. It just indicates that you haven't spent enough time in the future yet. Keep practising, it will become easier with habit. Charles Kettering, an inventor and a business consultant, said:

" *My interests are in the future, because I'm going to spend the rest of my life there!* "

Practise spending your time thinking about your future until it becomes easier to make the images appear clearly in your mind. This is something you can do at any time, such as when you're driving to work or just before you go to sleep.

That brings me neatly to my next point. You may know what you want to happen in your future history but the images may still not come through clearly. Again, don't worry about it. Trust me, you will get the hang of it with repeated practice.

For example, Robin Reid, the 1992 Olympic boxing bronze medallist, tells of how he and his fellow Olympic athletes repeated this exercise. They didn't sort of, kind of like, see themselves, you know, sort of winning the race or the event. They saw it in microscopic, minute detail. And they rehearsed it over and over until they could hold perfectly and play it back repeatedly, like a DVD.

Spending time thinking about your future is also a great opportunity to find out what *not* to do. If you find yourself failing to get excited by something you have always thought you wanted to do, maybe that is trying to tell you something? Lots of people say that they have always wanted to run a marathon. You may be one of them. However, when you were talking about it, did you find yourself imagining the moment you cross the finishing line after 26.1 miles and feel your heart beat a little quicker with excitement? Or did the thought make you feel only dread? It may be that you need to practise your ability to see your future history, but if you continually have a feeling of dread, then maybe this isn't the goal for you. If you don't have the energy or enthusiasm to make something happen, forget it! Use your energy for another goal that does make your spine tingle.

Former US President Clarence Day said about his own goals:

" *You can't sweep people off their feet if you can't be swept off your own.* "

You must repeat the future thinking exercise as often as possible, because the technique works by strengthening the mental pathways in your brain that are involved in making the action happen. It is like walking across a field. The first time you do it you leave only a faint pathway of where you tread, but if you walk along the same pathway two or three times a day, the pathway becomes stronger and clearer.

After the Rugby World Cup Final in 2003, Jonny Wilkinson was asked whether he was nervous when he received the ball to execute his last-second winning drop goal. His response:

" *No. I've been here a million times before.* "

He had used the techniques of future reflecting and continually imagining success many times before he actually took the kick.

Action

Go back to your SMART goal and start to run your own movies in your mind. Imagine yourself successfully achieving your goals and then do your best to think about them in really clear, precise detail as often as possible.

You can repeat this exercise whenever and wherever you want. The more you do it, the more likely your goal is to happen. As psychologist Émile Coué said:

" *When your will comes into conflict with your imagination, your imagination will always carry the day.* "

Brian Higginson

In December 1997, my wife, Christine, had noticed a lump that had developed in her breast and she went to Clatterbridge Hospital to get it checked out. The doctors did what is known as a fine needle aspiration, followed by a biopsy; when the results came back, the news was good. She was given the all clear.

Christine, however, wasn't entirely convinced and in April 1998 she was still worried as she noticed that the lump had begun to change shape. She returned to the hospital and had the lump surgically removed. After the operation, the doctors did some analysis but assured Christine that they were 99.9 per cent certain everything would be fine.

We waited for the results to come back . . .

That June was the summer when England were playing in the World Cup finals in France. Christine and I had saved up some money to go to the USA with the kids and were planning to visit Universal Studios, Disneyland, and all of the other sights. After the normal, early years of struggling to bring up young kids (we had two sons, Alec who at the time was 14 years old and George, 12), everything was beginning to look rosy.

Also at this time I was studying for a engineering certificate, along with a work colleague. This meant that I had to go away for a two-week course that involved staying away from home. During the first week I'd been keeping in touch with Christine every day, chatting and checking about the usual stuff ("How are you? How are the kids?" and so on).

On the first Thursday of the course, I nipped up to my hotel room during the lunch break to ring home. I knew that Christine had had an appointment in the morning at the hospital and so I obviously wanted to see what the news was. I didn't get an answer. At the time I thought that was a bit odd as I would have expected her to be back. I rang again at the end of the day, which was about 4.30 p.m., and still got no reply. When I rang again at about 6 o'clock I finally got through. Christine answered the phone and sounded a little subdued.

"I've got it," she told me quietly. "I've got cancer."

I felt myself go numb. I was shocked, to say the least. In fact, I'd go even further . . . I was absolutely devastated. As the words started to sink in, I became very upset.

"I'm coming home," I told her, but Christine would have none of it. She told me, in no uncertain terms, "Don't you start whingeing. I've got the problem and I will deal with it."

That evening, I just didn't know what to say or do. The lecturer had arranged a curry evening, followed by a walk into town with the other delegates and the enjoyment of a few drinks. I felt empty and gutted, but forced myself along to the restaurant, where I pushed the food around my plate, quickly made my excuses and left. That evening, one of the first thoughts that entered my head and remained was: "If I lose Christine, how will I cope with the kids?" Talk about selfish!

The other delegates came and met me in the bar after they'd finished their meal. They could sense that there was something wrong and so I told them the news, which cast a shadow over the whole evening. In those circumstances what can anybody say? The lecturer advised me to give up on the course and get myself home and someone immediately offered to drive me back. When I look back now and think about it, I realize that the telephone conversation I had with Christine was just the beginning of her fight with the "Big C". I told my course mates what Christine had said: "There's no point coming home tonight; I'll see you tomorrow."

When I got home on the Friday, I spent the weekend with Christine and we sat and discussed what was going to happen next. She was to have an operation the following Friday and she was very positive that she would get through this thing.

"Don't give up on the course. Go back, take your exams and pass!" she encouraged me.

On the Thursday, she went to the hospital to prepare for the following day's operation. On the morning of the procedure, a nurse came to see her and began to explain that the registrar wanted to have a word with her. The registrar carefully explained the surgery that was available in these circumstances. She could opt for either:

- a lumpectomy, i.e. removal of the tumour
  from the breast with a small amount of surrounding tissue; or:

- a mastectomy, which is the removal of all or
  part of the breast, sometimes removing surrounding muscles and lymph nodes.

Christine was dumbfounded when the registrar asked her what she would prefer. "Just get rid of the lot," she told him.

I got home from Stratford-upon-Avon that evening and went up to the hospital. When I arrived on the ward, the nurse pointed to where I would find Christine. She was fast asleep and looked so peaceful, I didn't have the courage to wake her. In fact, I just wanted to run away from the place. I told the nurse that she was asleep and I would have left it at that and gone back home. The nurse turned me around and told me to wake her up. I quietly called to Christine and when she awoke, she smiled. After what she'd been through, I couldn't believe how she could find it within herself to do that!

With cancer, things have to get worse before they can start to get better. After the operation, Christine went to see the consultant to discuss what further treatment was necessary. He told her that she required six months of chemotherapy and radiotherapy. During this visit, he also told her that the situation was worse than they had initially thought. Christine was diagnosed as having second-stage cancer and cancer cells had been found in her lymph nodes, which were also removed during the operation. We had gone from being 99.9 per cent certain that there was no problem to this diagnosis.

This was the beginning of the long haul.

At first, it seemed that Christine was all right. She'd go along to the hospital and they'd put the tubes in and then administer the chemotherapy. However, as time wore on you could start to see the toll it was beginning to take on her. She was becoming increasingly weary and nauseous. The chemo really knocked the stuffing out of her, but she was so determined to beat this thing.

A couple of years later, she told me about a radio programme she had listened to about a person who was also suffering with cancer, and about how that person had focused on the affected part of their body and "thought it out". Christine told me that she had literally lain in bed in the dark and thought about exactly where the cancer was and that she had willed it to disappear.

To have to endure chemotherapy is bad enough at the best of times, but to have six months' worth is even worse, and I could see Christine starting to fade away before my eyes. We have a photograph that was taken at New Year and, although she never completely lost her hair, you can see that it had thinned out and she looked really gaunt. The treatment never stopped her, though. She used to say that she was a mum and she wouldn't let this thing interfere with her being a mum!

After being poisoned for six months, because that's exactly what chemotherapy does to you, Christine was prescribed an anti-cancer drug (tamoxifen) which she would have to take for the next five years. The problem for women who suffer from cancer at this stage in their life (at the time she was 44 years of age) is all the "extras" that you get from the chemotherapy. Apart from the tamoxifen, she also has to take calcium supplements every day, for the rest of her life, because the chemo gives you a nice little helping of osteoporosis. And as if having cancer isn't bad enough, she then had to cope with the onslaught of the menopause . . . and I mean onslaught! The sensation that she got from this was tantamount to having her insides burning her up. At first, Christine would meet with a consultant and he'd check her out every three months after her treatment. When she asked him if there was anything she could take to help her with the menopause, the consultant said, "Sorry, but no. HRT can't be administered to you because of the cancer and so I suggest, to combat osteoporosis, you take plenty of load-bearing exercise, such as power walking!"

What has happened since?

After five years, Christine was taken off the tamoxifen. The consultant still sees her on an annual basis and he will keep doing so for the next five years, because she had cancer at a young age, but the whole cancer experience has had a dramatic effect on her life.

At the time she was diagnosed she was working as a care assistant in an old people's home. She really loved the job and even in her spare time she would take the wheelchair-bound residents out for walks. Because of what had happened, she couldn't carry on in that line of work any longer. The holiday to the USA, which we had so looked forward to, was put on hold for 12 months. Another love of her life is gardening, but with the removal of her lymph nodes if she gets any scratches on her arms they swell like a balloon.

But has the cancer stopped her doing what she wanted to?

Not at all. After some hassle from insurance companies about her condition, we finally managed to get the kids to

America and we travelled along the west coast – from Las Vegas to San Francisco – where we did helicopter rides, visited the Grand Canyon, the works!

We've also spent three weeks in Vietnam, staying first in Ho Chi Minh City then travelling for three days down the Mekong Delta, where we crawled through the Cu Chi tunnels. There were six of us in the party that went down into the tunnels and the only one who made it the full distance, in the sweltering heat, at least 25 feet below ground, was Christine.

We've been back to the States on a city slicker- type holiday in the mid west: riding horseback, herding cattle, white-water rafting on the Shoshone river.

Next year, she's planning for us to go to South America for three weeks, visiting Brazil, Uruguay and Argentina.

She still continues to potter about in the garden, even though occasionally, when she gets a scratch, she has one arm that looks like Gandhi's while the other looks like Arnold Schwarzenegger's.

She also manages to get away on field trips with the local history group and if you ever are walking in the fields near our house, you'll see Christine power-walking like a demon.

However, there is one story that captures just what effect the cancer has had on our lives.

One of the big milestones for us was Christine's 50th birthday. She loves to drive and she'd never had a new car. I was determined that we should put this right. We went and had a look at some of the cars on the Vauxhall parking lot and she was eyeing up a Corsa.

"Do you really want that one though, Christine?" I asked her.

She told me "yes", but I wasn't convinced.

"What would you *really* like?"

She thought about it and then said that the one she'd really like was the Astra Convertible, which was in the corner of the lot.

"That's it then. Let's get it!" I told her.

You'll see her occasionally for two weeks of the year

CHAPTER 7

TURN WATER INTO WINE

" *Within you right now is the power to do things you never dreamed possible. This power becomes available to you as soon as you change your beliefs.* "

MAXWELL MALTZ, COSMETIC SURGEON AND SELF-HELP
AUTHOR (1899–1975)

Did you know that fleas can jump great heights? In fact, they can jump the equivalent height of a human jumping a house. If you have a dog that has ever had fleas, that fact shouldn't come as a great surprise. If you ever do catch a flea, here is a brilliant experiment to try with it.

If you put a flea in a jar and then put a piece of cardboard on top of it, despite being able to jump far higher than the top of the jar, once the flea bangs its head against the card a few times it will never again, in its whole life, jump higher than the height of the card on top of the jar. That way they are easy to control and you need never worry about them again. This is how they train the fleas in flea circuses.

What has this got to do with you and your beliefs, you may be asking. Bear with me.

Once you have got rid of their fleas, here's an experiment for dogs that is interesting to note. In the 1960s Dr Martin Seligman of the University of Pennsylvania noticed during an experiment involving some dogs that when they experienced any physical pain they just gave up and lay down, whimpering pain. He was fascinated by this and wanted to investigate further, so he carried out another stage to his investigations.

He put dogs into three groups, A, B and C. Dogs in group A were placed in a box and then given an electric shock. The dogs could stop the shock by pressing a bar with their nose and they learned to do this pretty quickly! Dogs in group B were placed in another box and were given a similar shock, but they had no way of stopping it. Finally, dogs in group C were placed in the box but were not given any shocks at all.

The next day, the same dogs were placed in a different box, which had a low barrier placed down the middle of it. One side of the box gave off an electric shock when the dogs were placed next to it but, by stepping over the low barrier to the other side of the box, they could escape the electric shock.

Guess what happened?

The dogs in group A (those that had been able to turn the shock off the day before) and group C (those that had not received any shocks) very quickly learned to step over the barrier and escape the pain of the electric shock. Group B dogs (the ones that couldn't control the shocks in the first part of the experiment) didn't even try to escape. Instead, they conceded immediately, lay down and whimpered. They believed that they had no control over events and gave up right away.

The sceptics amongst you may say, "But they're dogs, aren't they?" How many times do you think it takes humans to give up and succumb to similar levels of helplessness?

Dr Seligman wondered this as well, and so he tried a similar experiment where a group of volunteers were put into a room with eight doors leading out of it. All the doors were locked and then a deafening noise, like the sound of radio static, was played into the room. The volunteers all immediately scrambled to get out of the room but found the doors locked, so sat back down again and put up with the horrible noise. Just as they all sat back down, Dr Seligman went round and unlocked all of the eight doors. Over the next three hours, how many people got back up and tried the doors again, to see if there was any escape from the horrible noise?

None of them. They had learned to be helpless after just one attempt.

The point of these experiments is that we all have beliefs, which then drive our actions and behaviours to produce certain results.

When you talk about identifying your purpose in life and the goals you want to achieve, the beliefs you hold are the most important factor in achieving them. It is your own beliefs that decide whether you will be successful. The formula is simple: if you change the belief, you immediately change the behaviour and, therefore, you change the results you will enjoy.

Henry Ford was the pioneer behind the first mass-produced motor car. He had a clear goal – to make the car the mode of transport of the future – and he had to overcome a lot of initial scepticism. He remained true to his beliefs and didn't allow others to change them. He said:

If I had listened to what my customers believed they wanted . . . I would have made a faster horse!

It doesn't even matter if what you choose to believe is actually true or not. After all, you once believed that Father Christmas was real and your forefathers and ancestors once believed that the Earth was flat. If you do actually believe in something, at a deep, subconscious level, this belief will dictate how you behave, every minute of every day.

Talking of Father Christmas, think back to when you believed he was a real person. Do you remember how it affected your behaviour during December, when you believed that you wouldn't get any presents if you were badly behaved? This relates back to the formula:

beliefs = behaviour = result

In this case the result was presents from Father Christmas.

It is how you behave, on a regular and consistent basis, that decides the sort of results you get. Again, the formula is really simple. If you change the beliefs at one end, you change the results at the other.

As you go through life, many of the barriers and obstacles that stop you from being successful come from within your head. You create and set limits for yourself and then convince yourself that it's impossible to go beyond those limits.

Once these barriers are proven to be breakable, you often look back and realize that the barrier was self-imposed. It didn't exist in reality.

Homer Simpson understood this truth:

" *Facts are meaningless. You could use facts to prove anything that is even remotely true.* "

Let me offer you what I consider to be the most powerful example of how beliefs can affect results. This was a belief that humankind held and accepted as fact for centuries. Since humans started to be measured against the clock, no one had ever run a metric mile in under 4 minutes. On 5 May 1954, the world record for this distance was 4 minutes and 1.4 seconds. To run a mile in under 4 minutes was a barrier that many "experts" felt was impossible to cross. In fact, the British Medical Council "knew" that the human body couldn't run that fast.

The following day, a 25-year-old medical student called Roger Bannister ran a metric mile in 3 minutes and 59.4 seconds, a fraction of a second below the impossible barrier. What is most amazing about his feat is what followed it.

Within 46 days of Bannister breaking the record, a New Zealand athlete, John Landy, broke that record by running 3 minutes and 57.9 seconds. By the end of the year, two men – Bannister and Landy – had managed to break the 4-minute barrier in the same race. Astonishingly, by the end of 1957, just over two and a half years later, 16 runners had also gone on to beat the clock. The lid had been removed from the jar. By 1999, the world record for the distance had been lowered 19 times; to date over 955 athletes have run sub-4-minute miles, accomplishing what was formerly believed to be an impossible feat more than an amazing 4700 times.

Think about your own situation. What barriers are keeping you back?

Action

Successful people have radically different beliefs to most of the population. They know that beliefs act as powerful filters for how they experience the world. They understand that you don't believe what you see – rather, you see what you believe. If you believe that the world is a bad place, you will probably find enough evidence to convince yourself that it is. The question is not what is true, but what will serve you best in leading the life you want to lead.

1. Go back to your list of goals from earlier. Pick one of your goals. Now be as honest as possible and write down the obstacles that are stopping you achieving that. Next to these, indicate which obstacles you believe are really impossible to conquer and which ones you could overcome with some thought and effort. Be brutal and challenge your own thinking. Share the result with others and ask for their honest views on what is really impossible.

   Some examples of barriers you may be imposing on yourself are:

   - Time
   - Money
   - Location
   - My boss
   - My partner
   - Disability
   - Being too fat
   - Being too thin
   - Lack of confidence
   - No support
   - Laziness
   - Debts
   - Knowledge
   - Qualifications
   - Being a woman
   - Being a man
   - Lack of transport
   - Fear of failure
   - Worrying about others
   - Illness
   - Children
   - Religion

2. Buy a book about one of your heroes who has been successful and compare your beliefs with theirs.

CHAPTER 8

DECKCHAIRS ON THE TITANIC

" If you wish to know your past life, look to your present circumstances. If you wish to know your future life, look to your present actions. "

BUDDHIST SAYING

Two factors determine how you spend your time. There are the things that are classed as urgent ("I must do it and I must do it now!") and there are things that are classed as important: actions that contribute towards your goals. When you know this, you can start to allocate your time and activities into four main categories:

1. Fire fighting (activities that are urgent and important).

2. Fire prevention (activities that are important).

3. False alarms (activities that are urgent).

4. Fire escapes (activities that are neither urgent nor important).

Let's look at each area in detail, as this will help you to plan your time better and assist you in achieving the goals you have identified.

Fire fighting

When you are fire fighting you are reacting to the world around you, like when the phone is always ringing, or your boss is angry and demanding action, or the production lines are always going down, or the kids are crying.

If this sounds familiar and you think you are spending a lot of your time in this area, it is likely to be because you are not prioritising effectively.

By the way, if you think this is your preferred style of operating, just ask yourself: how many fires are you responding to and how many fires are you actually responsible for starting? Some of the best fire fighters are also the best arsonists, as they enjoy the feeling of always being active and available to help. The question is whether you are putting your energies into the right areas, those that contribute to your goals.

Fire prevention

The more time you spend preventing fires, the less time you have to spend fighting fires and dealing with urgent and important issues. This is because you are planning, training, innovating and heading problems off before they become raging infernos. These issues don't depend on you getting involved and tackling them. You have to act first, to anticipate and solve them.

A great example of this is given in Sir Clive Woodward's book *Winning!*. He writes about the last seconds of England's World Cup win and he studies every pass, every move and every thought the players took in those crucial, dying seconds of the 2003 Final. He was able to identify every area of innovation, practice and planning that he and his coaching team had adopted over the previous six years, in anticipation of that very moment when Jonny Wilkinson kicked the winning points.

He didn't wait until he was in the heat of the moment or decide to leave anything to chance. Instead, he deliberately spent a large amount of his time in the "fire prevention" box and had accounted for every possible eventuality, including the requirement of a last-second winner!

One great example of fire prevention was Sir Clive's introduction of a training method that he called T-CUP

(Total Control Under Pressure). This is a technique that is taught to the elite soldiers of the SAS. Woodward had noticed that when the team failed to win their previous three Grand Slam matches, the players had lost all composure and control when they were chasing the game and they had reverted to a style that wasn't their normal approach and that played straight into the hands of their opponents.

T-CUP training involved putting his players in pressurized situations and then teaching them how to handle their own emotions and not to panic. In convincing his players of the benefits of this kind of coaching, he delivered a perfect example of prioritization.

He explained this by starting from the players' goal, which was to win the World Cup. If they lost control, they would lose their discipline. If they lost their discipline, they would lose penalties. If they lost penalties, they would lose points. If they lost points, they would lose games. If they lost games, they would lose the World Cup. When he explained it in these terms, the players all understood why they had to prioritize.

False alarms

False alarms are deceptive. Although they feel like you're fire fighting, you aren't. Events here feel as though they are urgent because of the noises of emergency and panic that people make. But on closer inspection, you find that the problem is usually a matter that is urgent to them alone.

Fire escapes

In fire escapes you find yourself doing anything, such as standing by the coffee machine, tidying the house or other easy distractions and excuses. You're rearranging deck-chairs while the *Titanic* sinks rather than doing what really needs to be done. Does this sound familiar?

Action

Life planning exercise

1. Think about the five most important things in your life. These may include your family, your parents, your career, your hobbies, your dreams and so on.

2. Now score these five things 1–10 on how happy you are with the amount of time you spend on them (1 = not happy; 10 = very happy).

(Continued)

3. Think about what you would like the ratings to be. Score your five important things 1–10 according to what you wish the time spent on them was (1 = much less time than currently; 10 = much more time than currently).

This exercise should give you a good indication of where you are spending most of your time. Is it in the areas you want? Think about what German writer Goethe said:

" *The things that matter most must never be at the mercy of things that matter least.* "

Where do you spend most of your time? Based on the goals you have set yourself, make a list of all of the actions you can think of that you need to take in order to achieve them. Work back from each final outcome, figure out the main steps you need to take before you can achieve your goal and write them down (remember the 3 per cent of Harvard graduates who wrote down their goals?). Can you take just one small step a day to get you nearer to your priorities?

CHAPTER 9

DO YOU SWIM WITH SHARKS OR DOLPHINS?

> " *Start each day with a smile and get it over with.* "

W C FIELDS, COMEDIAN AND ACTOR (1880–1946)

"There are men in your squad we wouldn't go into battle with," said the Royal Marines senior training instructor and rattled off their names.

"But why? What is it about them? They are clearly great at their jobs. Why wouldn't you go into battle with them?"

"It's not about their skills, Clive. It's about their attitude and their effect on the team. There are hundreds of soldiers who can run for three days, think on their feet and handle a weapon. But some aren't suited to working in a high-pressure team situation. It might be the smallest trait, like a moan when the going gets tough. One wrong team player can sap all the energy from a group."

This was a conversation between Clive Woodward and the trainer, after a team-building exercise that Woodward had arranged to discover who he should recruit to his team to go and win the World Cup. The Royal Marines trainer identified two groups of people in the team, Energy Sappers and Energizers.

The definitions of these terms are as follows:

Energy Sappers – like the verbs to bleed, deplete, devitalize, drain, erode, exhaust, undermine, weaken, wear down. Another way of thinking of them is probability thinkers.

Energizers – like the nouns drive, efficiency, exertion, fire, force, intensity, power, spirit, stamina, strength. Another way of thinking of them is possibility thinkers.

The thing is, not only do you become what you think about most of the time, you also become like the people who you spend most of your time with.

Educator Sir John Jones regularly speaks to newly qualified teachers and he cites one main factor that determines whether teachers are successful. It is not how well they know their subject or how well they can control a class – it is where they sit in the staffroom.

He challenges teachers to think about whether they sit with people who love their job, enjoy the challenge of teaching and love the lifestyle it affords them, or with people who love nothing more than to moan, gripe and bellyache about the job, the management, the canteen or the tea. Sir John calls this second group "dream snatchers", the people who haven't achieved their dreams and will stop you achieving yours.

Robbie Williams wrote a song about one of these dream snatchers, which he included as a hidden track on his *Life Thru a Lens* album. It was dedicated to one of his teachers who couldn't be bothered to learn his name for six years and who had laughed about his ambitions to be a pop star, suggesting instead that he join the army,

Hello Sir
Hello Sir, remember me?
I'm the man you thought I'd never be
The boy who you reduced to tears
Lad called "thingy" for six whole years.

Yes, that's right, my name's Bob
The one who landed the pop star's job
The one you told, look don't touch
The kid who wouldn't amount to much.

Well, I'm here and you're still there
With a fake sports car and receding hair.
Dodgy Farah trousers that you think are smart
Married to the woman who teaches art.

Married to the life, married to the school
I wanna sing and dance Sir; now who's the fool?
Sing and dance, you thought I was barmy
Settle down thingy, join the army.

And who are you to tell me this?
The dream I want I'll have to miss
Sir is God, he's been given the right
To structure lives overnight.

Now I know life's true path
Tanks and guns that'll be a laugh
No, not me I'm a mega civilian
I won't lead my life riding pillion.

But thanks for the advice and I'm sure it'll do
For the negative dickheads just like you.
As for now I've a different weapon
Stage and screen is about to beckon.

And here I sit in first class
Bollocks Sir, kiss my arse . . .

Jock Stein, the manager of Celtic FC who was the first British manager to win the European cup, agrees with the view that possibility and probability thinkers are able to determine your success. He said that the art of successfully creating a great player was to keep him away from the eight team mates who hated the manager and would poison his thinking, and to steer him towards the other two who haven't made their minds up yet!

Now think about yourself.

If you were to list the people who you spend most of your time with, would you describe them as probability thinkers? If you need help in identifying them, listen out for the typical comments that this sort of person specializes in:

> *It will be a disaster; it always is!*

Or, to quote Homer Simpson again:

> *You tried your best and failed miserably. The lesson is 'never try'.*

Are they the sort of people who boast about having twenty years' experience but could realistically be said to have had one year's experience that they've repeated twenty times? Are they people who respond to every idea with the words: "Yes, but . . . "? Are they the kind of people comedienne Victoria Wood had in mind when she said:

> *Man invented language only to satisfy his need to complain.*

If so, then you're surrounded by probability thinkers.

Or are you in the company of possibility thinkers? They typically comment, "Yeah, sounds good!"

These are people who look on the bright side and try to see the potential in everything. They respond to every idea with the words: "Yes and . . . ". Athletics coach Frank

Dick calls them "mountain people", because they love to rise to a challenge. Sir Isaac Newton, the man who defined the laws of gravity, referred to them in a letter to his friend when he said:

" *If I have seen a little further, it is by standing on the shoulders of giants.* "

Think about yourself. Are you a probability or a possibility thinker?

US sociologist Dr Wayne Dwyer believes that we all belong to a number of different tribes at home, at work and socially. Each tribe operates within certain guidelines and traditions. Some of these are necessary, as they make sure that the tribe survives, but many of its laws can hold the most talented people back, as the tribe moves at the speed of the slowest person and doesn't like one of its members learning something outside its laws.

Four-time Olympic gold medal winner Sir Matthew Pinsent explains how this occurs. He and his three team mates would be wired up to static rowing machines when training and the machines would check that they were all rowing at the same speed and with the same power. When they were all rowing in perfect harmony, the total result was that they were 110 per cent more powerful. If one of the team dropped his rate by a fraction, the other three would subconsciously drop as well, without even noticing. As Pinsent said:

" *With a tired or weak team member, a boat will only go as fast as he allows it to go.* "

The message here is that who you surround your-self with is just as important as your own mental approach.

The next time you are sitting in the canteen and find one of your mates telling you that a task is impossible or that you are wasting your time chasing after something you have identified as your purpose and goal, remember the following example of someone who refused to listen to probability thinkers. Unfortunately, these probability thinkers included the national government and a whole nation, who told him that things couldn't and wouldn't change, no matter what he said or did. He was regarded as a dangerous fool and was imprisoned for remaining a possibility thinker.

66 *Our deepest fear is not that we are inadequate. Our deepest fear is that we are powerful beyond measure. It is our light, not our darkness that most frightens us. We ask ourselves, Who am I to be brilliant, gorgeous, talented, fabulous? Actually, who are you not to be? Your playing small doesn't serve the world. There is nothing enlightened about shrinking so that other people won't feel insecure around you . . . And as we let our own light shine, we unconsciously give other people permission to do the same. As we are liberated from our own fear, our presence automatically liberates others.* 99

Nelson Mandela used those words by peace activist Marianne Williamson in his inauguration speech as pre-sident of South Africa.

Action

1. Identify which "tribes" you belong to. Make a list of the people you spend most of your time with:

   - at home

   - at work

   - socially

2. Now look at the people in these tribes and identify the probability thinkers and the possibility thinkers. Which group do you spend your time with?

3. Identify a group of people you admire, people you believe can help you achieve your goals and whom you can help achieve theirs. Commit to meet up and communicate on a regular basis to swap ideas and offer encouragement.

Liquid Thinkers

Gerry Fannon

How did I get started?

I was working as a service engineer and was doing a lot of travelling around the country. I was regularly working 90-hour weeks and one Friday, I was driving back home from London and took a short cut through some back country lanes, when I passed a boatyard. I don't know why I did, but I suddenly decided to stop the car. Like I say, I still don't know why I did it, but I parked up, got out and had a look around the different canal boats that were moored in the yard. Then, on impulse, I decided to hire one of the boats for a week there and then!

My first trip was a week's holiday on the canal boat with my wife and another couple of friends. We decided that we were going to sail to Market Drayton, in the Midlands, but we had a pretty inauspicious start.

We were given an hour's training on how to open the lock of the canal, but the training was given on a lock where the water level only rose and dipped by about 4 inches. Easy! After we had set sail, though, the first lock we came to was the major thoroughfare of two of the major canal routes in Britain, the Trent and Mersey with the Shropshire union. It was like learning to drive on a quiet, private, country road and then having your test on a motorway.

It will probably not surprise you to learn that we never did make it to Market Drayton, but by the end of that week my ability to steer and open the locks had improved massively. We were hooked. So much so that we booked another week's holiday for the year after and were determined to make it to Market Drayton.

When we returned, we enjoyed another great week and although my confidence at controlling the boat had improved, we still didn't make it to our destination. We did, however, so much enjoy the whole experience of being out in the countryside, enjoying the fresh air, watching the wildlife and finding hidden gems that you would never see from the roads, that we decided to save up and buy a canal boat, determined to fulfil our ambition of finally making it to the mythical land of Market Drayton. By the third year, we had our own boat and planned our trip in great detail, working out the route and everything else we needed to consider. It took us two-and-a-half weeks and the holiday was amazing and justified our decision to buy the boat. The biggest disappointment was that when we got to Market Drayton, it wasn't worth the effort! Think Ellesmere Port without the nightlife or excitement.

We kept the boat for seven years and had some brilliant holidays and memories on it. I also started to learn loads about the skills of canal boating. It was during these holidays that I started to think about what changes I'd make if I had the chance to build my own dream boat. Some of these were practical changes, such as making the engine easier to access, having central heating and improving the wiring and electrics. Some of them, though, were really radical. Most boats follow roughly the same design – they have a saloon, a kitchen, a bathroom and a bedroom. They all look the same and I knew that I wanted something different, something unique, something I could call mine.

I started going to the Ellesmere Port Boat Museum and began looking at the different styles of boats, which dated back some 200 years. I then started taking photos of different sorts of boats and taking ideas that I'd seen on one boat and thinking about how I could adapt it to another. I drew diagrams and models, dozens and dozens of them, just putting down ideas and thinking about what it would look like and how practical it would be.

I had already started taking photos of the boats and then did research at the library and on the Internet about the practicalities of my ideas. Let me give you an example. Most modern boats are made of steel, but I really liked the idea of how they used to make boats 100–150 years ago, which was to use planks of wood to construct the bow of the boat. I liked the idea that it would look old but would also be distinguished and unique.

Also, most boats have fairly basic facilities like a shower and a toilet. In my dream boat, I wanted a large bath and a power-shower. If you are stood on the deck all the day in freezing weather, I can't think of anything better than to thaw out with a long soak in the bath. So I drew that into my design.

Once I'd decided what I wanted my dream boat to look like, I found some guys who used to work at the Cammell Laird shipyard and showed them my plans and designs. They certainly thought that the boat was unique and had never built anything like it before. They agreed to have a go at it. However, before they would give their full commitment, they insisted on building a model of it in plywood to see that it was possible. Once they had reassured themselves, and me, that my design was possible, they gave me their agreement.

I then went along to the shipyard every week, whenever I got the chance, and made amendments to the design as I saw it starting to take shape. For example, I'd wanted the boat to have portholes fitted into the sides, but when they were in I realized that they didn't let a lot of l ight in and so I added Houdini hatches in the roof. Gradually, the boat started to take shape and began to look like my design.

The build didn't go without complications, though. I had a really clear idea of where I wanted the engine to sit. I wanted it to go in the same place as on a trawler. This required using lots of angles and guesswork to position it in the right place; I got

heavily involved at this stage and helped the lads
work backwards from where I wanted the engine.
After a lot of work, we finally managed to fit it
and I was very happy with the result, as it gave
me a lot more room. As the boat continued to take
shape, I carried on making amendments and
changing the design to fit in with the dream version and
the costs started to creep up. My initial estimate of
£25,000 ended up being dwarfed by the final amount of
£37,000. My wife and I were committed to the project,
though, and we knew that it would be worth it. We found
the extra funds.

The whole building project took over two years to
complete and on the day I collected my boat, I
arranged for it to be picked up by a low loader and
taken to the wharf, where it was going to be lowered
into the water by crane. By the time I'd made all the
arrangements and finalized things, I arrived at the
wharf and the boat was already in the water. It looked
beautiful. The time was about 5 p.m. and it was a
two- or three- hour trip to the marina where the
boat was going to be moored, so I decided I was
going to treat myself to a Chinese and a pint and I
eventually ended up falling asleep on the deck.
When I woke up, it was a lovely bright morning
and I set off to the marina. Once I was nearly there,
I gave my wife a call to tell her to get there so
she could see the boat arrive. When she answered,
she didn't seem too pleased to hear from me. It
was 6 o'clock in the morning. I'd been so excited,

I hadn't checked the time but had got up at 4 o'clock to set off!

I can remember, exactly, the moment I knew that all of the planning, preparation, saving and hard work had been worth it. It is crystallized in my mind.

We had gone to walk the dogs along the towpath and I looked back and saw my boat sitting among a number of others, all moored up. I remember thinking that if I were a passer-by, I would have picked out my boat as the one I would have wanted. "That's our boat," I said to my wife. It looked classy.

I'd like to live on the boat eventually and enjoy long cruises on it, to places like Oxford and Skipton. I have an ambition to take it to the Albert Docks, when the canals there are re-opened. It would also be amazing to travel in it along the canals and lakes of Ireland. The thing is, though, I will always be working to improve it. Every time I get close to completing it, I start planning some other improvement.

What advice would I give to others?

You should know what you want to achieve and you should write it down and go back to it again and again to check that it is what you really want.

You should read up and do as much research as possible on what you want to achieve. You will be amazed at the range of ideas you can find. For example, in the 12 years since I started canal boating, technology has moved on in leaps and bounds and this research has allowed me to project my thinking forward and build it into my dream boat.

I'd also encourage you to fit your dream into the context of your whole life. This will allow you to decide how important your goal is to you and help you understand exactly why you want it. If you wanted to have your own canal boat for holidays only, you may not spend as much money or invest as much time into it as I did.

Finally, I urge you to enjoy learning an amazing amount along the way. I never dreamed that I'd acquire the skills I have, but the experience has been great fun.

CHAPTER 10

STOP WHALING

" *My dear friend, clear your mind of can't.* "

SAMUEL JOHNSON, ESSAYIST AND THE COMPILER OF THE
FIRST DICTIONARY OF THE ENGLISH LANGUAGE (1709–1784)

I recently read an article that explained that William Shakespeare had used 17,676 different words in his plays. He was responsible for inventing over 1,700 new words, such as critic, laughable, swagger, envy, elbow room and moonbeam. If you think this book contains the "naked truth", you're using a phrase he created. On the other hand, if you think "it's all Greek to me", well, that's another of Shakespeare's creations.

To show that anyone can invent a word or phrase, football manager Sir Alex Ferguson coined "squeaky bum time" for the pressure that players and managers feel at the end of a season. Iain Dowie, Crystal Palace manager, has also found his way into the dictionary by describing the ability to respond to setbacks as possessing "bouncebackability"!

This idea of being able to invent words and phrases got me thinking. If something can be created and put into a dictionary, then surely words can also be removed. Right?

One lesson all successful people share is the ability to take the word "failure" out of their vocabulary and then behave like it doesn't exist. Ellen MacArthur, the youngest person and the fastest woman to sail around the world single-handedly, said:

66 *Successful people usually snap success from seeming failure. If they know there is such a word as defeat or failure, they will not admit it. They may be whipped but they are not aware of it. That's why they succeed.* 99

If failure doesn't exist for you, you can't fear it, can you? James Dyson first had the idea of inventing the bagless vacuum cleaner back in 1972, yet you couldn't buy one in the UK until 1992. What was he doing for the 20 years in between? Let him explain:

> *Failure seldom stops you. What stops you is the fear of failure. I have never encountered it, as I have only ever had temporary setbacks. Never walk away from these setbacks. On the contrary, study them carefully – and imaginatively – for their hidden assets. If you want to double your success rate, double your failure rate.*

After he had finished his playing career, footballer Jimmy Greaves was asked to explain how he had achieved the record of scoring 49 goals in a season for Tottenham Hotspur. He said:

> *I also got another, less well-known, record that same season. I got the record for the highest number of goals missed. I got this as I understood the lesson that I couldn't score every time I had a shot but I definitely wouldn't score, if I never even tried.*

Golfer Greg Norman had the same attitude. In 1996, after losing the US Open to Nick Faldo despite leading the field for the whole tournament, Norman was expected to sneak away quietly, but instead he chose to face the whole world's media to explain:

> *Losses aren't a waste of time. They are an apprenticeship. Real failure is a man who has blundered and not cashed in on the experience; failure is an attitude not an outcome.*

Here's a question for you: Do you ever talk to yourself?

As you read this book, listen to the voice in your head that you can hear now. This is what psychologists call your "self-talk".

Here is another question for you: Do you speak to your friends and family in the same way you allow the voice in your head to speak to you?

If you answered "yes" to this second question, answer a third: Do you have many family or friends left who still speak to you?

On average, you talk to yourself around 10,000 times a day. How many of the things you say to yourself are positive messages and how many are negative? How many times do you find yourself saying "I can't do that" or "I'm an idiot"?

This voice in your head, your self-talk, is the key to making you a success and helping you achieve your goals.

Studies have been carried out with children whose parents are working in professional industries and others whose parents are on social security benefits. Up until the age of 4, the children from professional families will have received 700,000 positive comments, such as "well done" and "excellent", and only 80,000 negative comments, such as "stop it" or "don't do that". In contrast, children from families on benefits will, by the same age, have received 60,000 positive comments compared to 120,000 negative ones.

So the "professional kids" hear seven times as many positive comments as negative ones, whereas "benefits kids" hear twice as many negative statements as positive ones. This statistic is a huge factor in determining how successful a child will be in later years.

The great thing is that it's never too late to stop and reverse this kind of attitude. Ask yourself again, what is the proportion of positive to negative comments you tell yourself every day?

Try this technique. Start to monitor what you say to yourself and substitute phrases like "I won't" for "I can't". Can you see the distinction between the two? We're back to the whole matter of choice, which is where we started this book. Stop telling yourself "I'll try" and instead tell yourself "I'll choose to/choose not to".

Think of Yoda, the wise old Jedi master, who when Luke Skywalker expressed doubts about his ability to beat Darth Vader and conquer the Dark Side, told him:

" *Do or do not. There is no try.* "

This reminds me of a story told by England international footballer Jimmy Meadows about a technical course he once attended in a factory:

" *A positive something is better than a negative nothing. There were several operators and engineers present for this course and the instructor radiated positive thinking as he spoke and thought, only in terms of the impossibility of failure and the certainty of success.* "

"We were given a test in what we had learned so far and, as we did it, one or two of us began to discuss the problems we had encountered. The instructor wasn't having any of that and he said: 'Let me make one thing perfectly clear, gentlemen. In the world of TPM there are no such things as problems, only opportunities!'

"There was a pause and then one of the guys in the far corner said, very gently, 'In that case, I wonder if you would give me a hand with an insurmountable opportunity?'"

Start to change your own language.

Action

Since 80 per cent of your emotions come from how you talk to yourself, make yourself accountable for your internal dialogue.

1. Start to monitor what you say in your head and then make yourself a promise that you won't say anything to yourself that you wouldn't allow a stranger to say to you.

2. Count how many times you say out loud that you "can't" do something or how useless you are and then aim to reduce the number.

3. Train yourself to ask better questions, rather than asking yourself why you can't do something or beating yourself up for not achieving something. Think about a situation where something has gone wrong for you and ask yourself the following questions:

- How important will this be in a couple of months' time?

- Is my response appropriate to the situation?

- Can I improve or influence this situation?

- Can I find anything positive in this situation?

- Can I learn anything from this situation?

- Would I do anything differently next time?

Practise asking these questions next time you are faced with a similar situation and notice how doing so starts to affect the results you get.

CHAPTER 11

GO FISHING

"Striving for excellence motivates you; striving for perfection is demoralizing."

HARRIET BRAIKER, PSYCHOLOGIST AND MANAGEMENT
CONSULTANT (1948–2004)

You are never going to get everything right first time. Did you know that according to business guru Tom Peters, the Sony Corporation takes about five days to go from having an idea to having a product to test in the marketplace? Compare this to most companies, which on average take 11 months to achieve the same thing.

Why is there such a difference? It would appear that Sony is not chasing perfection. It is looking for feedback, which it can take and build into its next efforts.

Don't aim for perfection. Give yourself permission to be imperfect.

Just as important is the question of who you choose to listen to. Look back to the earlier chapter about whether you associate with possibility or probability thinkers and think about the people you surround yourself with. Manchester United manager Sir Alex Ferguson claims that he takes advice from everybody, but rarely uses it unless it comes from an achiever:

> " *By achiever, I don't necessarily mean someone who has scored a mountain of goals or won every trophy available. I don't care which path they have gone down, so long as they've done the walking. That way, you know that they know the consequences – the price. People who know those things rarely talk rubbish.* "

It is critical to go fishing for feedback from people who will give constructive criticism rather than false praise or damning dismissal. Avoid what former US President Theodore Roosevelt called "those poor spirits, who neither enjoy much or suffer much because they live in the grey twilight that knows not victory nor defeat".

Virgin Group owner Richard Branson has identified the people who matter to him – his customers – as an important source of feedback:

" *Whenever I'm on a flight or train or in a record store, I ask people for their ideas on how to improve the service. I write them down and when I get home, look through what I've written. If there's a good idea, I implement it.* "

Ask for regular feedback and take it from those who matter.

Action

Keep track of your progress and how many attempts you make at achieving your goal. Don't claim: "I must have tried 100 times to improve or change things." Count whether it was actually only once or twice before you gave up.

Share your goals with other people and ask for feedback in as many forms as possible (written and verbal) from as many different people as possible as regularly as possible.

Finally, practise being gracious in your response to feedback. Make it easy for people to offer you their opinion.

Paul Lee

What is your ambition? That's a good question, isn't it, and it's only since I sat down to contribute to this book that I have had a chance to think about my answer to this question.

How did I go from being a raw 19-year-old football player to being a well-respected rugby club captain successfully delivering a speech to over 200 colleagues? It was a hell of a journey! Let me tell you a bit about it and what I learned along the way.

I was a pretty good footballer and had even had trials for Everton. I was playing twice a weekend and once during the week. It was during the summer closed season that I decided to go along to my local rugby club, Old Instonians, just to keep fit, in anticipation of the football season starting again.

A lot of the training involved loads of running and at this stage I had, quite literally, never picked up a rugby ball before. After I had been going along to the fitness sessions for a few weeks, one of the blokes running the training asked me whether I fancied joining in the practice games. I'm a big lad anyway, and they thought that I could stand in as a second row. After a bit of persuading, I agreed to give it a go. I actually enjoyed it more than I thought I would. I carried on going along to the training and joining in the games until, eventually, they asked me if I'd like to play for the 3rd XV.

I still regarded myself as a footballer first and foremost, but I agreed to play for the Old Instonians and help them out where I could. So for a few years I fitted in playing rugby around my football commitments. It was only when I got to 21 that I finally understood and knew exactly what I wanted to do and achieve in rugby.

I got invited along to one of the club dinners and I can vividly recall seeing the club captain stand up, at the top table, and deliver a fantastic speech to a packed audience. What really sticks out in my mind was the respect he seemed to command from everyone in that room. I looked around me and saw the faces of people rapt at what he had to say. I noticed that the banter, which is always pretty near-the-knuckle at these dos, was tinged with a real respect towards this guy.

I knew, there and then, that if I was going to carry on playing rugby, I didn't want to be just a rugby player. I wanted to go one step further and become a rugby club captain.

In rugby, the role of the captain is really different from in football. You are responsible for selecting the team, for giving the team talks, deciding the tactics and hosting the other teams when they visit you and acting as the ambassador for your club when you visit others. It is more similar, in lots of ways, to the role of a manager of a football team. You are responsible for setting the tone of the behaviour and attitudes within your club. The position is regarded as a real honour and a privilege. To be given it, you must be elected by the players and the committee members. They must believe you have the sort of qualities to carry out these tasks, as well as being good enough to make sure you are selected for the 1st team.

If you'd asked me at this stage – remember, I was still only coming along for a laugh and was still trying to learn how to play the game – how I was going to become a member of the 1st team, let alone captain it, I wouldn't have had a clue. It is only now, with the benefit of hindsight and experience, that I can recognize what motivated me. It was the picture of imagining myself as captain, exuding respect and self-confidence, that motivated me towards what must have looked like a pipe dream.

How did I manage it, then? I carried on the commitment of coming along to the training sessions and I kept on improving my skills in the second row and listening to the help and advice the other players gave me, until I made it into the 1st XV. Over the next few years, I managed to establish myself as an important part of this team and kept on improving my game by regular practice and hard work.

The club captaincy is held for two years and before the current captain had to stand down, I spoke with my mates and they agreed to support me when I stood for election. I put myself up and was awarded the position. This wasn't enough, though. I wanted to feel like I could achieve the levels of respect and credibility that I had enviously felt years earlier, and I knew that it would take me a while longer to get this.

There were times when the role was tough and I considered packing it in. One example stands out. In my first year, there was a lot of backbiting and moaning about selection issues and so I had to close the dressing room doors and have some blunt conversations with the team. I put an end to the complaining and we started to work together as a team. In later years, friends of mine have told me that my honesty and my willingness to face up to these issues really started to help me become established and achieve the respect I craved.

You may read this and think that my ambition is a bit vague, because it was centred more around a feeling than something you could measure, but I can remember the exact moment when I knew that I had got there and knew that I had managed to get the status I had wanted so badly from that first club dinner.

Over the next few years, I had moved to different clubs a couple of times and was elected as club captain on both occasions. I was playing for Old Parkonians against my other old team, Prenton. In rugby there can be a lot of funny business (punching, gouging, biting, that sort of thing) which goes on in the rucks and the mauls. On this day, during that game, none of this went on. There were no underhand methods and it was played in a really hard but fair way. We won and the opposing captain came up to me afterwards and admitted that we had given them a real beating. There was a real respect, which I felt that my old team had given me, in accepting that it would be tough but in not resorting to cheating. The feeling of knowing that I had gained that level of respect was amazing and gave me a real thrill.

What did I learn that I could pass on to anyone else about going for your ambitions?

There are a couple of pieces of advice. The main one is that you will have doubts about whether you can do it, but the reality of a situation will very rarely be as bad as your doubts.

Secondly, I'd say don't wait for chances to come along. Go for it. Nine times out of ten you will get an answer of some sort or another, which will help you move forward towards your goal.

Finally, remember to enjoy what you're doing along the way.

CHAPTER 12

THINK IN WATER COLOUR

" *We are not retreating, we are merely attacking in another direction.* **"**

MAJOR GENERAL OLIVER SMITH (1893–1977), US MARINE CORPS, DURING THE BATTLE OF CHOSIN RESERVOIR IN THE KOREAN WAR

There are no rules for creativity. Here are five guidelines that lead to fresher, more innovative ideas.

Go for quantity

"I find that the best way to have a good idea is to have lots of idea," remarked US chemist and pacifist Linus Pauling, winner of the Nobel Prize for Chemisty and the Nobel Peace Prize.

When it comes to creativity, more is definitely better, partly because you never know when you are going to hit on something great and partly because by going for volume, you force yourself to think more widely than just about your immediate problem.

Don't judge or evaluate ideas as you go along

This is the hardest rule to stick to. No sooner do you have some seemingly absurd thought than you dismiss it as, well, absurd. All ideas are good ideas, because at the time you have them, you don't know where they might lead you.

Capture all the ideas you have in some way

If you don't write your ideas down, you may end up concentrating on just trying to remember what you've already thought of, rather than putting the ideas, however brilliant, to one side and thinking afresh.

Learn to love half answers

The moment of genius may come from letting an earlier thought that you liked (but couldn't quite put your finger on why you liked it) take shape and form in your mind. Ambiguity is great. Don't dismiss partial solutions as they can often lead you to the complete answer, even though, frustratingly, it may not be straight away.

Be naïve

Even the most experienced panel of experts can miss the answer to a dilemma precisely because they are applying their experience. They are able to identify all of the complex difficulties obstructing their normal procedure – but by being naïve in your approach, you may be alert to the existence of another approach altogether.

One story that captures this point perfectly is the classic tale of the lorry that got stuck under a bridge. A crowd gathered and offered several solutions. Some suggested tearing the top off the lorry, others said dismantle the bridge. The argument raged back and forth until a small child at the back asked: "Why don't you let the air out of the tyres?"

Have an objective

This is the most important point and relates back to the purpose of this book. Aimless creativity is usually just that. Always keep in mind your sense of purpose, as this greatly increases the odds of you coming up with something that is not only original but also worthwhile.

Many inventions we take for granted today had the strangest of beginnings. For example:

- The roll-on deodorant. Deodorant was invented back in 1888 in Philadelphia, but it wasn't until the 1950s that the roll-on appeared. The inspiration? The ballpoint pen. An inventive employee worked out that the same idea could be used to spread the deodorant evenly.

- The microwave oven. This invention came about as a by-product of Second World War radar research. While working on magnetrons (vacuum tubes that produce microwave radiation), engineer Percy Lebarron Spencer discovered that a chocolate bar in his pocket had melted. Working out that the microwaves were the cause, he experimented and discovered that not only could microwaves cook food, they could do so much faster than a normal oven.

- The alcopop. This was invented because an Australian farmer was throwing away a large proportion of his lemon crop, simply because the lemons weren't the right size. Rather than letting these rot, his neighbour, a brewer, took them and used his knowledge of brewing and a family recipe for lemonade, and the Two Dogs lemon brew was created.

If you always do what you've always done, you will always get what you've always got. Be creative in your journey towards your goals.

Action

Answer these two questions:

1. Were you a kid once?

2. Do you dream?

The answer to both questions is "yes" and they prove that you are both creative and innovative.

Think of the daydreams you used to have as a kid during the long summer holidays. For example, you may have dreamt of playing for your favourite team at Wembley in a cup final. Make a list.

What do you dream about now? In an earlier chapter – Are you a drifter? – you answered what you would do if you won the lottery. Look back at the list.

You may dream that you would travel the world if you suddenly became rich. Now start to be creative and think about where and how you could travel without being a millionaire!

Finally, go back to your goal, which you wrote down in the **Liquid Go(a)ld** chapter. Write down as many ways you can think of to achieve it. Apply the creative principles detailed above. The answer will be out there, you just need to think about it creatively.

CHAPTER 13

SWIM AGAINST THE TIDE

" *Nothing in the world can take the place of Persistence. Talent will not; nothing is more common than an unsuccessful man with talent. Genius will not; unrewarded genius is almost a proverb. Education will not; the world is full of educated derelicts. Persistence and determination alone are omnipotent.* "

CALVIN COOLIDGE, 30th US PRESIDENT (1872–1933)

Research into sales has shown that 73 per cent of customers say "no" five times before they say "yes". Further studies demonstrate that only 8 per cent of salespeople ever go past being told "no" five times or more. Do the sums. This means that 8 per cent of people are getting 73 per cent of the business, so no wonder they go on to become the most successful people in an organization. It is the same with you and your dreams. How many of us just give up the first time we get a "no"?

Perseverance is not about doing the same thing over and over. It also requires the courage to look at yourself and change your habits.

In the days when the only cars Ford sold were open-topped Model Ts, all the dealers in America were told to close during the winter. Henry Ford, the head of the company, reasoned that they wouldn't be able to sell open-topped cars at that miserable time of year. During the winter break, he decided to do a tour of his most successful dealers to see whether he could offer any help or advice for when they re-opened in the summer. Ford arrived at his most successful dealership – a place that sold twice as many cars as its nearest rival – during a heavy snowstorm. He was surprised to find it open. He summoned the manager and asked him what he thought he was doing, selling cars in the middle of the winter. The manager replied, "Sorry, Mr Ford, nobody ever told us we had to close."

Now you have identified your purpose and your goals, as you begin to move towards them you may not see any results immediately and so you may start to feel that they are not worth pursuing.

Frank Dick, who coached tennis player Boris Becker, runner Linford Christie and decathlete Daley Thompson, was the head coach of the British track and field team throughout the 1980s. It took a long time before they tasted any success and then the team won the European Cup in 1989, the first time a British team had achieved this.

When journalists asked Dick how he had done it, he explained that it was down to the preparation and work done years before. He used the story of the Chinese bamboo:

" *The Chinese bamboo plant, when it is planted, doesn't do anything in the first year. It doesn't even sprout a single green shoot; nothing. It is the same in the second year. And the third year and the fourth, yet, in the fifth year, in a space of 6 weeks, the bamboo will grow to be over 90 feet high. The question is, did it grow 90 feet in 6 weeks or in 5 years? It proves that persistence does pay off.* "

Harrison Ford was in Hollywood for 14 years and was working as a carpenter before he was offered some acting work. He commented:

" *It took me 14 years to become an overnight success.* "

The actress and model Sophia Loren spent many similar years facing rejection and being advised to quit and get a normal job. She said:

" *Getting ahead requires avid faith in yourself. You must be able to sustain yourself against staggering blows and unfair reversals. When I think back to my first years in Rome, those endless rejections, without a glimmer of encouragement from anyone, all those failed screen tests and yet I never let my desire slide away from me, my belief in myself and what I felt I could achieve.* "

Another great example of persistence is Spanish cyclist Miguel Indurain. The first time he rode the Tour de France, he finished 90th. The next year he finished 40th, then 19th, then 10th. By the 5th year he finally won the race and he continued to do so for the following five years. He says:

" *Within us all is a message which we tend to overlook: most of us have highs and lows but it's the perseverance, the determination, at the day's end that makes us what we are. It is not about being smarter or having more opportunities, as others will tell you. Those who won't take the risk of failing and go for it, who won't see things out, they're the ones who come home early, never answering the challenge and never going anywhere.* "

When you have committed to your goals, rejection will inevitably come your way. Expect it. Welcome it. Cherish it. Then ignore it and carry on.

Action

Commit to being unstoppable. Tell yourself, every day, that you are unstoppable.

What made Stuart Pearce take a crucial penalty for England in Euro '96 when he had already experienced the pain of missing one six years earlier against Germany, which saw his team lose the semi-final? Pearce says that he had banished his fear of failure and so was prepared to take a risk in order to dare to be successful.

This fear makes us stop taking risks and start playing conservatively and small. As Marianne Williamson puts it: "Why should you not be brilliant, gorgeous, talented, fabulous?"

Think of an example of where you have exceeded your own expectations.

Make a promise to yourself to become unstoppable – and keep it.

Liquid Thinkers

Steve Byrne

When I was a young lad, I worked alongside an older guy who used to speak about his goal of building his own home but never got around to doing it. This was when the idea took hold and stayed in the back of my mind, but it was never something that I'd discussed seriously with anyone, not even with Karen, my wife. When I look back now, this thought was obviously still there in my mind when we were looking around for a house in 1996. This was one of my life-long ambitions and I had a chance of making it happen.

When we saw one place, it looked like the Addams family house it was so desperately run down, but there was something about it that made me go back and look beyond the surface and consider its potential. It had a huge plot of land attached that provided us with some scope to build on it. After a bit of thought, we went ahead and purchased the house and moved in that year. Even at this point Karen was not aware of what I had in mind and what I was planning.

By 2001, our second daughter Alicia had been born and the house was starting to feel too small for a family of four. Our elder daughter, Charlotte, had started at a good school and was really enjoying it and we wanted both of them to be educated there. Unfortunately, the local council had implemented a restriction that meant you had to live in the local area to qualify for a place there. The house prices in that area were pretty steep and so we had a clear choice: either find the money to move to the area or uproot our elder daughter so that both of them could go to the same school. We didn't want to take the second option, as my girls' education is of the utmost importance to me. It seemed as good a time as any to bring up the idea that had been germinating in my mind for years and I suggested we build a house on our plot of land, selling both, which would allow us to generate the cash to move to the appropriate area. We had to do this by 2005 if we were to achieve our aims. Things didn't turn out to be that simple.

I spoke to Karen and we agreed that we had a powerful reason to want to do it. There were only two real problems:

- I had no experience of building and didn't have a clue about where to start.

- We didn't have any spare money.

We decided to go ahead with our plans anyway . . .

The only asset of any value I had was my beloved motorbike and I put it up for sale to signal my serious intent to the family. We used the money to pay for an architect to draw up plans. We all got involved in helping to design the layout of the house. It looked fabulous and we excitedly submitted it to the council for the necessary planning permission.

Bombshell no. 1 was that we received a rejection letter, politely explaining that we had a Tree Preservation Order on an old oak tree that proudly stood at the bottom of the garden. We were undeterred and went back to the drawing board with our architect and re-submitted our revised plans. The response was a little more encouraging. The council said that if we could receive confirmation from a tree surgeon that the oak tree wouldn't be damaged by the building work, we could go ahead. I was watching the money from the sale of my bike being quickly eroded, but the tree surgeon confirmed that our plans were sound. We got back to the council, who insisted that we pay for its tree surgeon to double-check. Twelve months had passed by the time we had found our way through this bureaucratic maze.

The next stage of our plan was pretty simple. We needed to borrow £100,000 from a finance company. This would allow us to build the shell of the house. After this, I would take responsibility for building the rest of the place, including fitting out the whole of the interior. We went round quite a few companies and were met with a lot of refusals. Bombshell no. 2 was that one or two of them suggested we needed to sell the house we were living in to raise the money. This wasn't an option. Not only did I not want to disrupt the family, we didn't actually have anywhere to move to in the interim. We needed to build the house before we could sell our current home. It was a "catch 22" situation.

It was September 2003 before the Nationwide building society agreed in principle to lend us the required amount, as long as we were able to show it costings, plans, insurance and a welter of other documents to prove that we knew what we were doing. It felt like we were on our way!

I had already started discussions with the builders we planned to use and they explained that unless they started building work in October, it was likely to be another six or seven months before they would be able to fit us in again. In addition, they explained that as winter was approaching, we needed to get the foundations down before the poor weather set in. I didn't have the final approval from the Nationwide but the building society had given me its agreement in principle. I had to balance the options. We couldn't afford to delay the building work if we were to meet our 2005 deadline, but we didn't have the final approval for the funding. I can still remember the date when I crossed the Rubicon. It was 18 October 2003 and I came home from work to find a bloody big JCB digger churning up my garden and I knew that there was no going back. Besides, the approval from the building society would be arriving any day.

However, a couple of weeks later I got a third bombshell, a phone call from the Nationwide explaining that it had lost my application. I had to re-submit all of the information again and face another month-long wait for approval. In the meantime, I had to find £10,000 to pay the builders for the first month's work. I chased around and arranged a short-term loan from my bank.

It was the week before Christmas when I finally heard back from the Nationwide. The guy on the phone cheerfully informed me that the building society wouldn't be lending me the money and he helpfully added that he didn't think there was a bank in existence that would lend us the amount we needed. As he was speaking, the image of that JCB digging my garden up danced before my eyes. I was poleaxed.

I recovered myself and managed, somehow, to put a brave face on for the sake of the girls, so that they could enjoy Christmas. I kept thinking about where I could find some positives from the mess I was in. The only comfort was that the builders had taken two weeks off for Christmas and so I didn't have to pay them. I was in too deep to go back, but I lay awake at night, a feeling of panic rising up in me. Karen began to recognize the fear I was feeling. She suggested that we back out completely and call off the builders. It was tempting, but I was determined to find a way around the problem and continue. The resulting stress caused conflict in our marriage.

It was a chance conversation with my sister-in-law in the bleak January of 2004 that offered a slim glimmer of hope. She works for the Halifax and she mentioned that she knew a friend of a friend who might be able to lend us the money. By this time the amount I had borrowed to pay the men working on the house had risen to £57,000 and the interest payments from various bank loans were starting to spiral out of control.

The Halifax agreed to lend the money on the proviso that the Abbey, the company with which I had a mortgage on my current property, agreed to split the land. The Abbey sent a surveyor round to value the land to see if it was worth more than the mortgage I held with the bank. If this surveyor said "yes", I would get my loan. If he said "no",

I was in serious trouble with no obvious way out. This marked the start of the longest, most sleepless and stressful week of my life. When the letter dropped through the letterbox in March 2004, I hesitated briefly before I dared to open it. I knew that I was holding more than a letter in my hand. I was holding £58,000 worth of spiralling debt, a half-built house, land and an existing house that were seriously devalued, and a marriage that was coming under severe strain – and all because of some idea that I'd been incubating for years. When I finally opened the letter, the relief flooded over me like a wave. It said "yes". I had a quiet moment alone where I thought that we must have used up our share of bad luck by now.

The building work could continue and we got the shell up in three months. We then got the first house on the market in order to pay back the loans and it sold within a week. I started to think that our luck had begun to turn. We agreed a completion date of August, which gave us a three-month deadline to transform the shell to a condition we could live in. I had a target and I threw myself into it. I'd come home every evening, get changed and work until it turned dark, seven days a week, furiously driving myself on to complete the work. Every spare minute I was engrossed in working on our home. I learned how to carry out the plumbing installation and I assisted in the work on the electrics, plastering and flooring.

A significant moment, which had a deep and lasting effect on me and my attitude, came one Saturday. I was hammering away while my daughters were playing with their friends in the sand downstairs. I could half hear their conversations and I caught one of Charlotte's friends comment: "I wish my daddy could build a house." My eldest daughter's reply stopped me dead. "You wouldn't, Beth," she said. "I don't see my dad." I stopped what I was doing and lots of thoughts went through my mind. I remembered my dad, who had worked at Levers for 40 years – the last 15 of which were working nights – and remembered how much I had missed him and I thought, "What have I done?"

I realized that in my desire to reach my goal and build a dream house, the whole family had suffered, especially my wife, who had never complained but had continued to support me and keep the family moving without my help. That day, I resolved to myself that when I had finished this house, I would make up to Karen and the girls for my months of absence.

While this was all going on, I was helping my parents move house. During this period my dad suffered a heart attack. It seemed like one thing after another. Where would it end?

Immediately after we had sold our current house, we paid £1000 to a company to arrange to have all of the services – gas, electricity, water etc. – installed. The waiting list for this is about three months and that fitted neatly within the timescales we were working towards. In the October, however, we received a phone call from the management of this company. They were deeply apologetic, but the agent we had been dealing with had just been dismissed for fraud. He had taken our money but had made absolutely no arrangements to have the services fitted. We faced another three-month wait and we suddenly had no home we could live in, as we had to move from our current house within the week or face huge financial penalties for breaching the contract.

We ended up moving into my mother-in-law's house, where the girls had to sleep on the floor in sleeping bags while we were cramped in a small box room. During the three months we stayed here, the girls would continually ask when we could go home. I just felt so helpless. It was a nightmare.

In December 2004, just before my deadline of 2005, we eventually moved into the newly built house and had another couple of tough weeks when we had to borrow water from the neighbours until we had our own supply fitted. We decided that after everything we had been through, we should live in the house for at least 12 months before facing the stress of another move.

At the same time, my youngest daughter was allowed to move to the school we wanted, which removed the pressure of having to move home immediately. My dad recovered fully from his heart attack and both he and my mum moved into their new home, where they are happy and settled. Most importantly, my relationship with my family is now stronger than ever. Before, I would sit and read a magazine and have a ready excuse for the kids if they wanted me to go and play with them. Now, I think back to that day when I heard the hurt in Charlotte's voice and enjoy getting up and playing with them. Karen and I have been through so much stress and turmoil, we now know that there is nothing we can't deal with together. And what about me? I sometimes allow myself a long soak in the bath and time to reflect on the great sense of pride and belief that building the house around me has given me. It gives me a real, deep sense of satisfaction. I have learnt so much, including the knowledge that nothing can stress me out any more – as well as the deep-rooted belief that I can attempt anything, if I really want it enough.

Karen asked me if I'd had a crystal ball back in 2003 and could know what would happen over the next two years, would I have still gone ahead with it? My answer was an undoubted and resounding "yes". My purpose was to be the best dad and husband I could possibly be and my goal – to build a house for the family – was very clear. If you know your goal, there is nothing – not illnesses, lies, setbacks or overwhelming odds – that you can't overcome with belief and persistence.

CHAPTER 14

DIVE IN!

“ *Knowing is not enough; we must apply.*
Willing is not enough; we must do. ”

GOETHE

There are two ways to climb a tree:

1. Climb it.

2. Sit on an acorn and wait for it to grow.

Now you have identified your purpose, written your goal, committed to it and fallen in love with it, do something, however small, that takes you a step in the direction of achieving it.

Time does not wait for any of us. Don't wait for circumstances to be perfect.

    " *Tucked away in our subconscious is an idyllic vision. We see ourselves on a long trip that spans the continent. We are travelling by trains. Out of the windows we drink in the passing scenes of cars on nearby highways, or children waving at a passing crossing, of cattle grazing on a distant hillside, of smoke pouring from a power plant, of row upon row of corn and wheat, of flatlands and valleys, of mountains and rolling hillsides of city skylines and village halls.*

"But uppermost in our mind is the final destination. On a certain day at a certain hour, we will pull into the Station. Bands will be playing and flags waving. Once we get there so many wonderful dreams will come true and pieces of our lives will fit together like a completed jigsaw puzzle. How restlessly we pace the aisles damning the minutes for loitering waiting, waiting, waiting for the Station.

'When we reach the Station, that will be it!' we promise ourselves. 'When we're 18 . . . win that promotion . . . put the last kid through college . . . buy that 450SL Mercedes-

Benz . . . have a nest egg for retirement!' From that day on we will all live happily ever after.

"Sooner or later, however, we must realize that there is no Station in this life, no one earthly place to arrive at once and for all. The journey is the joy. The Station is an illusion – it constantly outdistances us . . .

"So gently close the door on yesterday and throw the key away. It isn't the burdens of today that drive men mad, but rather the regret over yesterday and the fear of tomorrow. Regret and fear are twin thieves who would rob us of today. 'Relish the moment' is a good motto . . .

"So stop pacing the aisles and counting the miles. Instead, swim more rivers, climb more mountains, kiss more babies, count more stars. Laugh more and cry less. Go barefoot oftener. Eat more ice cream. Ride more merry-go-rounds. Watch more sunsets. Life must be lived as we go along. The Station will come soon enough.

Source: "The Station", Robert J Hastings

Personal postscript

I have always wanted to write a book. I wasn't bothered what sort: biography, fiction, sci-fi, real-life stories, it didn't really matter. I just loved the idea of sitting down alone and translating my thoughts onto a piece of paper. I had never even given any thought as to who would bother to read my words. It was the concept of writing that appealed to me.

I can now recognize that this was the problem. There was no purpose to it. If I didn't know what I would write about, let alone who I would write for, where was the motivation to do anything about it?

Over the last few years I have thought about writing a book quite a bit and have even become eloquent about my intention to write. In fact, it is one of the first topics of conversation with my wife, Geraldine, when we go away on holiday. You know those first few days when you start to unwind and enjoy getting used to the fact that the days are your own, to fill however you want? Well, this is normally the moment when I come back to one of my favourite topics, writing a book. I have sat in cafés, bars and restaurants from the balmy beaches of Copacabana to the frozen landscapes of Reykjavik and bored Geraldine with my intention that this was the holiday when I would start to put pen to paper. She has even learned the art of silencing this looped conversation by challenging me with the question: "What will you write about?" I tend to mumble a reply of "Er, I'm not sure" before quickly changing the subject.

I started work in Port Sunlight in May 2004 as the Human Resources Manager for North West Liquids.

During my first few weeks, I had the chance to spend some time helping out and getting to meet some of the people who worked on the lines and in the warehouse. During break times, we would chat about our weekend, hobbies and families, and I noticed that there was one common thread that ran through every conversation. Everyone I spoke with had a passion, something they cared deeply about and enjoyed.

I met one lad who was a keen bodybuilder. It turned out that he competed at the sport. I don't know the first thing about bodybuilding, but when we started chatting I began to appreciate the different characteristics that were required for it. You needed discipline in order to get up and go training three or four times a week; you required a high degree of analysis to be able to judge your diet accurately enough to come into competition looking your best. Finally, to put yourself up against others must require a healthy level of competitiveness. What I also noticed was that when we spoke the lad came alive, bubbling with enthusiasm and passion. He cared about his sport. He wasn't the only one.

As I started to get to grips with my job, I remembered the conversations I had enjoyed in my first few months and thought that if only we could do something that could tap into those depths of passion, skills and characteristics, we would be able to improve the performance in the workplace. After all, if you are doing something that you think can help or support your passion, you are more likely to care about it and do it well. It struck me that doing something was within my command.

At the start of the year, I launched a Training Academy in the factories. My aim was to offer everyone the opportunity to develop themselves in some way and help them to be brilliant at their job. I also wanted to offer the chance to meet others who were brilliant at their chosen profession, so I started inviting a guest speaker to come in every month and talk about their career and how they had successfully achieved their goals and ambitions.

It didn't matter how diverse each speaker was, because there were a number of common characteristics and techniques that they all employed on their journey to success. Karen Darke, a woman who was paralysed at 21 before she cycled across the Himalayas, identified the need to possess a clear goal, as did Robin Reid, a world champion boxer who was drawn to the sport to achieve self-respect. Sir John Jones, the headmaster who turned around Britain's worst school, recognized the need to change his and his pupils' beliefs regarding their own ability as much as Chris Moon had to when facing up to his disability. Fergus Finlay, the man responsible for bringing the Special Olympics to Ireland, echoed other guests in acknowledging the importance of persistence.

As I started to see the common threads, the idea for my book started to emerge as a realistic opportunity. It had all of the right ingredients. I wanted to write a book, I was passionate about the subject matter and I enjoyed researching and reading books, plus it could be unique and special due to the rich resource I had exclusive access to – the people within the factories.

As I began to capture the themes that bound all of these achievers together, I recognized that I should also adopt them. If I was going to write about something, I should be able to say, with all honesty, that I had also employed the same techniques. This book is testimony to the principles that are contained in it.

I knew that I had previously lacked focus about writing and didn't have a target. This time, I wrote my goal down on a postcard. I then put the postcard in my diary and used it as a bookmark. I knew I would see it every day and that it would motivate me to take at least one step a day that moved me closer towards my goal. What I wrote down was:

> *" I have written a book about personal success and the techniques to achieve it. I have used lots of examples from famous achievers in order to make and highlight the points but have interweaved stories of my colleagues amongst it, to demonstrate that these techniques are open and available for us all to use. I have published it in December 2005. "*

I wrote to people whom I regard as heroes or achievers in their own chosen fields and asked them for their opinions on what techniques and characteristics were present when success happened. Tony Smith, a legendary rugby league coach, focused on the importance of adopting a positive attitude and gave up time to sit and discuss his experiences with me. Sir John Jones discussed the characteristics he had recognized in his years of teaching and helping to salvage desperate situations. My dad, who is a world-class boxing trainer, and his fighters gave their views on the difference between success and failure.

More great advice and support came from an unlikely source, a visit to the doctor's. I sat in the waiting room, flicking through the magazines that were on display, and I read an article about Bill Sweetenham, which detailed his approach to bringing success to Britain's swimming teams. I wrote his name in my notebook and I resolved to contact him. Amazingly, just over a month later, I bumped into Mr Sweetenham at Glasgow Airport and I explained what I was doing and asked him for his help, support and opinions. He agreed to come and meet with me and has offered a number of insights and views for the book.

Sir Winston Churchill once said, "It is a good thing for an uneducated man to read books of quotations." I have always tried to take that advice on board. When I read a book, I do so with a notebook nearby. I am a collector of quotes and stories that I can use either in work or in coaching. Once I had identified 14 of the most important techniques for achieving success, I included in this book the stories, anecdotes and facts from my reading. It's funny, but once I knew what I was looking for, I started to see loads of other examples in every walk of life (a great example of my RAS working) such as in films, magazines, interviews and adverts.

In the course of my job I have met a number of fascinating people who have told me their stories. I approached some of them, explained my purpose and invited them to contribute. It staggered me that everyone I asked was so eager to help and offer up their stories with honesty and candour. They made me feel inspired in the evenings when I came home and couldn't face sitting down to write.

I knew that I needed to show my work to others and get feedback. I asked Geraldine to give me her honest assessment and she was as good as her word. Unfortunately, I wasn't quite prepared for such honesty and felt incredibly protective as she made a number of constructive criticisms. Eventually, we agreed on a compromise; she would continue to read the drafts and give feedback, but I would listen and consider what she said for a few hours before responding. 90 per cent of the time I accepted her comments and made the changes, but it taught me an important lesson about myself and about feedback. I had to adjust my thinking to be able to accept it.

When you are clear about what you want to achieve, an incredible number of opportunities will present themselves. For example, I attended a course about organizational design. What could possibly be of benefit to my book about such a course? However, during it an incredibly talented cartoonist produced fantastic illustrations. I was amazed and fascinated by his brilliance and approached Andrew Park, who agreed to illustrate and design my book.

Finally, I wanted to get a Foreword for this book from someone like Muhammad Ali, an icon who embodies a lot of the techniques it contains. How was I, writing a book in my spare time, ever going to approach someone like Ali to help me out? I started from my goal and worked backwards, thinking about how I could reach it. My dad knew a man who knew a man who knew Angelo Dundee, Ali's trainer and coach throughout his boxing career. I wrote to him explaining everything, and he agreed to write the Foreword on behalf of himself and Ali. If you're going to dream, make it a big one.

Ultimately, if you have read up to this point in the book, I want to offer you my sincerest thanks for being a part of my dream (and sparing Geraldine any more of those annoying holiday conversations). If you do follow the principles here and they help you achieve your dreams, please tell me about it. That will be an affirmation of my purpose, which is where we started this book . . .

Thanks for reading. Now it's your turn.

Damian Hughes
Manchester, April 2009

Recommended Reading

Terry Anderson, *Den of Lions: A Startling Memoir of Survival and Triumph* (Ballantine Books, 1994)
Anderson was an American who was held hostage in Lebanon at the same time as Brian Keenan and John McCarthy. His story is equally compelling. He is a man who invested his faith in natural justice and believed that he would be freed as he had done nothing wrong, and his dignity and faith are astounding. I once met Anderson, who maintains that we could all survive his ordeal as "we do not know just how capable we are until forced to prove it".

Lance Armstrong, *It's Not About the Bike: My Journey Back to Life* (Berkley Trade, 2001) and *Every Second Counts* (Broadway, 2004)
Two books that should be on every school curriculum. The first details Armstrong's upbringing and how this forged his love of cycling and competition, then covers his fight with cancer and how he beat the disease and went on to win his first Tour de France. The second book is about his life after this and the longer-term impact of cancer on his life and the lessons and changes it has brought about. Brilliant.

Patrick Barclay, *Mourinho: Anatomy of a Winner* (Orion, 2005)
A fascinating profile of football manager José Mourinho, looking at how he started out in coaching and refined his skills along with his mental approach to become one of the most successful modern-era coaches.

Jean-Dominique Bauby, *The Diving Bell and the Butterfly* (Vintage, 2007)

This is the story of a man who suffered from a massive stroke and then came round to find himself suffering from a condition known as "locked-in syndrome". His only method of communication was to move his left eyelid. This book is amazing on a few levels. First, Bauby wrote it by spelling out every letter. Secondly, it's a book that describes in rich, evocative detail the simple things that we take for granted. Beautiful.

Wayne Bennett, *Don't Die with the Music in You* (ABC Books, 2002)

A short book written by a legendary Australian Rugby League coach, which touches on sport, life and the values that inspired him to success.

François Bizot, *The Gate* (Vintage, 2004)

The harrowing account of man who was captured by Khmer Rouge soldiers in Cambodia yet emerged to become to powerful intermediary in the country's civil war.

David Bolchover and Chris Brady, *The 90 Minute Manager: Lessons from the Sharp End of Management* (Prentice Hall, 2006)

A great book containing a lot of research into how football can provide lots of lessons for the world of work.

Sir Richard Branson, *Losing my Virginity: The Autobiography* (Virgin Books, 2007)

A good book describing how Branson built up his business empire, along with great insights into the attitudes and beliefs that have made him so successful.

Bill Capodagli and Lynn Jackson, *The Disney Way: Harnessing the Management Secrets of Disney in Your Company* (McGraw-Hill, 2006)

A book that describes how the Disney empire was established and how it has adapted to maintain its success today.

Bill Capodagli and Lynn Jackson, *The Disney Way Fieldbook: How to Implement Walt Disney's Vision of "Dream, Believe, Dare, Do" in Your Own Company* (McGraw-Hill, 2000)
A series of exercises that Disney uses to train its staff.

Dale Carnegie, *How to Win Friends and Influence People* (Vermilion, 2007)
This is an old book (first published in 1936) but is regarded as a classic. It has lots of tips and advice about how to work effectively with others.

Rubin Carter, *The Sixteenth Round: From Number 1 Contender to Number 45172* (Penguin, 1999)
"Hurricane" Carter was a potential world boxing champion until he was given life imprisonment for a murder he maintains he did not commit. This book tells, in graphic detail, about his brutal upbringing in young offenders' prisons, his subsequent fight for justice and how he fought for his beliefs.

Barbara Cassani, *Go: An Airline Adventure* (Time Warner, 2005)
A great book that covers the start-up of the budget airline Go and how it involved and inspired its staff.

Michael Crick, *The Boss: The Many Sides of Alex Ferguson* (Pocket Books, 2003)
This is a great counter-balance into Ferguson's own account of his life and times. It presents others' insights, both good and bad, into Ferguson and his qualities.

Mihaly Csikszentmihalyi, *Creativity: Flow and the Psychology of Discovery and Invention* **(HarperCollins, 1996)**

A book detailing the science behind creativity.

Frank Dick, Winning: Motivation for Business, Sport and Life (Abingdon Publishing, 1992)

This is a short book written by one of the best sports coaches of the last 30 years. Frank Dick uses his experience of coaching the cream of British athletics to provide insights into how these lessons can be used in our own lives to succeed in what we want to achieve.

Angelo Dundee and Mike Winters, *I Only Talk Winning* **(McGraw-Hill, 1985)**

The book by Muhammad Ali and Sugar Ray Leonard's trainer offers some great insights into the mentality required to be a success in both the boxing ring and in life.

Eamon Dunphy, *A Strange Kind of Glory: Sir Matt Busby and Manchester United* **(Aurum Press, 2007)**

The best biography of Sir Matt Busby ever written. This book offers a great view into Busby's vision of a successful football club, which upheld his own values of honesty, ambition, excitement with the accent on developing young talent, along with his attempts to create it. These values are still steeped in the core of the club today.

Marc Elliot, *Walt Disney: Hollywood's Dark Prince* **(Andre Deutsch, 2003)**

An alternative view of Disney, based on a lot of research on the upbringing that helped shape his character.

Dominique Enright, *The Wicked Wit of Winston Churchill* (Michael O'Mara, 2001)

A series of quotes from Churchill. Worth having to hand for if you ever find yourself short of something to say.

Harold Evans, *They Made America: From the Steam Engine to the Search Engine* (Little, Brown, 2004)

A book about America's pioneers and the creators of inventions that have shaped the modern world.

Michael Finnigan, *They Did You Can: How to Achieve Whatever You Want in Life with the Help of Your Sporting Heroes* (Crown House, 2007)

A collection of fascinating interviews with everyday people who were inspired to achieve their own goals. If you have enjoyed my book, you will love this one.

Alex Ferguson, *Managing My Life: My Autobiography* (Coronet, 2000)

Whatever you think of Ferguson, you can't deny his passion, ambition, drive and fierce will to win along with his values of loyalty and commitment. This book explains how these were formed and helped him achieve unprecedented success.

Victor Frankl, *Man's Search for Meaning* (Rider & Co., 2004)

Frankl survived the Nazi concentration camps. This is a powerful and moving book of what he learnt and I'd advocate that everyone reads it.

Thomas Hauser, *Muhammad Ali: His Life and Times* (Robson Books, 2004)

One of the best biographies of all time. This is the most comprehensive account of Ali's life you could find. Read about his rise to become world heavyweight champion, his refusal to go to Vietnam, his re-emergence as champ and his life after boxing. This book is brilliant.

Chris Heath, *Feel: Robbie Williams* (Ebury Press, 2005)

Absorbing journalistic biography of the pop singer, charting his life and career.

Michael Heppell, How to Be Brilliant: Change Your Ways in 90 Days! (Prentice Hall, 2007)

Does what it says on the cover! A book that offers advice on how to reach your goals.

Napoleon Hill and W Clement Stone, *Success Through a Positive Mental Attitude* (Pocket Books, 2008)

Stone built $100 into a multimillion-dollar organization and he describes the techniques he used to achieve this.

Brian Hughes, *Starmaker: The Untold Story of Jimmy Murphy* (Empire Publications, 2002)

The definitive book on Jimmy Murphy, Sir Matt Busby's assistant. Packed with anecdotes about how Murphy's revolutionary coaching and motivational techniques helped to nurture the finest collection of footballers ever, the "Busby Babes". This is a book written by my hero about one of my heroes.

Spencer Johnson, *Who Moved My Cheese? An Amazing Way to Deal with Change in Your Work and Your Life* (Vermilion, 2002)

Lots of home truths told within a story about two mice searching for cheese. Sounds unusual? It is, but worth a read.

Roy Jenkins, *Churchill* (Pan Books, 2002)
Biography of Britain's great war-time leader. It is a compelling book.

Roger Kahn, *A Flame of Pure Fire: Jack Dempsey and the Roaring 20s* (Harcourt Brace, 2000)
An excellent book that looks at the social implications of early twentieth-century America and the Depression that saw the emergence of Jack Dempsey, a lad who grew up homeless and without a base and became the world heavyweight champion.

Brian Keenan, *An Evil Cradling* (Vintage, 1993)
This is one of my favourite books of all time and Keenan is one of my ultimate heroes. He was taken as a hostage in Beirut in the mid-1980s and held for five years. In the book he describes how, despite having his basic needs denied, he managed to retain his values of honour, respect and dignity.

John Keith, *Bob Paisley: Manager of the Millennium* (Robson Books, 1999)
Similar to the Eamon Dunphy book on Busby, this is a comprehensive study of Liverpool's most successful manager and gives a great insight into his values and beliefs along with his determination to maintain the success he enjoyed.

Joe Lovejoy, *Sven: The Final Reckoning* (Harper-Collins, 2004)

A biography of the England football manager, covering his early coaching career in Sweden and Portugal.

Ellen MacArthur, *Taking on the World* (Penguin, 2003)

Autobiography of the youngest and also the fastest woman to sail single-handedly, round the world. MacArthur tells her story with real honesty, sharing her fears and doubts, which allows the reader to get a real understanding into the mind and motivation of someone who possess certainty about what she wants and how she is going to get it.

Archie Macpherson, *Jock Stein* (Highdown, 2007)

A brilliant biography of Scotland's greatest manager, Alex Ferguson's hero. Imagine a team winning the European Cup with 11 local lads. This book explains how Stein made this happen.

Nelson Mandela, *A Long Walk to Freedom* (Abacus, 1995)

Fascinating insights into how the African leader maintained his dignity and channelled his anger into finding a solution to apartheid.

John McCarthy and Jill Morrell, *Some Other Rainbow* (Corgi Books, 1994)

John McCarthy was held as a hostage with Brian Keenan for four of the five years he was in captivity. His story is equally amazing, as he retains his own quiet dignity in the face of horrendous circumstances. His then partner Jill Morrell campaigned to get the British government to act for his release. This is a brilliant book showing just how powerful passion and belief are and how they can sustain you beyond what you believe are your own limits.

Steve McDermott, *How to Be a Complete and Utter Failure in Life, Work and Everything: 44½ Steps to Lasting Underachievement* (Financial Times/Prentice Hall, 2008)

A fantastic and compelling book, which is packed with facts, anecdotes and philosophies told in an easy-to-read and conversational style that, if you ignore and disregard, can help you succeed in failing!

Paul McGee, *S.U.M.O. (Shut Up, Move On): The Straight-Talking Guide to Creating and Enjoying a Brilliant Life* (Capstone, 2006)

A fun and illuminating book that provides a no-nonsense set of tips.

Mind Gym, *The Mind Gym: Wake Your Mind Up* (Time Warner, 2005)

This book captures a lot of the information found at the website of the same name. It is best read in sections and is packed with lots of easy-to-understand scientific data that explains our behaviours and attitudes and has loads of tips about how we can improve.

John Monie and Tom Mather, *The Iceman: The Story of the Most Successful Rugby League Coach Ever* (Mainstream Publishing, 2002)

A fascinating book about the life and coaching expertise of the legendary rugby league coach John Monie.

Bob Monkhouse, *Just Say a Few Words: Complete Speaker's Handbook* (Virgin Books, 2004)

A brilliant book by the late comedian, which contains loads of tips about public speaking, including an excellent chapter on how to handle your own doubts and self-talk before standing up at an important event. Plus, it's got loads of funny stories, anecdotes and one-liners.

Chris Moon, *One Step Beyond* (Macmillan, 1999)
This is the inspiring story of a man who believed he could make a difference. After leaving the military, he went to Cambodia to help clear landmines and was captured by Khmer Rouge rebels. He later went to Mozambique and was blown up by a mine, losing his leg and arm. Within a year of this he ran the London Marathon and within three years he had run across the Sahara Desert. An amazing testimony to the power of the mind to overcome the steepest odds.

Naomi Pasachoff, *Linus Pauling: Advancing Science, Advocating Peace* (Enslow Publishers, 2004)
A biography of the two-time Nobel Prize winner. Pauling was an activist against atomic weapons and was subsequently accused of being a communist and suffered persecution, yet maintained his beliefs in spite of huge pressure.

Norman Vincent Peale, *The Power of Positive Thinking* (Vermilion, 1990)
More practical tips that provide you with the tools to carry out your ambitions and hopes.

Matthew Pinsent, *A Lifetime in a Race* (Ebury Press, 2005)
A revealing sporting autobiography that offers insights into the mind of the athlete. Pinsent talks candidly about his own doubts and fears and how he dealt with them to win four Olympic gold medals.

Christopher Reeve, *Still Me* (Arrow Books, 1999)
This book by the former Superman actor recounts his tragic horse-riding accident and tells his life and career story up until then in a series of flashback sequences. There are some heart-breaking descriptions of how he came to terms with suffering from complete paralysis and being unable to breathe without support. His determination to defy doctors and learn to walk again, in order to be able to play with his young son, is an amazing testimony to the power of belief. Although he didn't walk before his death, he did successfully gain funding into research and pioneered many techniques that will one day enable others to walk again. It is inspiring and very motivating.

Anthony Sampson, *Mandela* (HarperCollins, 2000)
The definite biography of Mandela. Offers comprehensive views of him from others' perspectives.

Joe Simpson, *Touching the Void* (Vintage, 1998)
An awesome story of survival in the mountains. This book has become regarded as a climbers' classic.

Ragnar Sohlman, *The Legacy of Alfred Nobel* (Bodley Head, 1983)
The story of how the inventor of dynamite chose to leave a legacy that was intended to celebrate and help secure peace.

Nobby Stiles, *After the Ball* (Coronet Books, 2004)
This is an excellent book by Stiles, a World and European Cup winner. He describes how he battled against huge odds to become a footballing legend, while maintaining the values he grew up with. Inspiring and illuminating.

William Taubman, *Nikita Khrushchev* **(Yale University Press, 2000)**

Authoritative biography of the Russian leader, who had the courage to condemn Stalin.

Jack Welch, *Jack: Straight from the Gut* **(Headline, 2003)**

The autobiography of the head of GE. An excellent book written in a down-to-earth manner, which makes it really accessible to everyone.

Richard Wiseman, *The Luck Factor: The Scientific Study of the Lucky Mind* **(Arrow Books, 2004)**

Explanations of the science behind what can sometimes appear to be random or lucky events, with lots of tips about how you can also become lucky.

Clive Woodward, *Winning!* **(Hodder Paperbacks, 2005)**

This book really appealed to me as it combined the world of sport with lessons that can be adapted and applied to the workplace. Don't let Woodward's subsequent failure with the British Lions and his transfer to football put you off. There is a great deal in this book from which anyone can learn.

Zig Ziglar, *Raising Positive Kids in a Negative World* **(Thomas Nelson, 2001)**

A must for all parents. Packed with lots of tips, help and advice about raising kids and about seeing the very best in them.

Afterwords

If you have enjoyed this book, you are in good company.

Nobby Stiles is one of only two Englishmen to have won the World Cup and the European Cup. The other is Sir Bobby Charlton.

I am honoured to be asked to write a few words for this book and I hope that it provides you with some insights and inspiration which will let you go on and achieve your dreams and ambitions, just as I achieved mine by playing for Manchester United, winning the European Cup in 1968 and winning the World Cup with England in 1966.

I grew up in the back streets of Collyhurst, Manchester and my poor eyesight, lack of height and slight frame made me possibly the least likeliest contender to ever achieve footballing fame. I did it, however, through a combination of knowing what my dream was and never losing sight of it, no matter how tough times got, and by having a fierce determination to succeed. Without these attributes, all of the skill in the world wouldn't have helped me and it is for this reason that I'd encourage you to read this book and have a go at the exercises that are at the end of each chapter.

I would have loved the chance to read a book that could have helped me take a step closer towards my ambitions when I was younger and you should also make the most of the chances which are offered to you in this book.

On that famous day in June 1966, just before extra time in the World Cup Final, Sir Alf Ramsey told us that we had the chance to step forward and achieve our ambitions over the next 30 minutes. We met the challenge that day and this book presents you with the same opportunity to understand and achieve your own ambitions. Make sure you take it.

Nobby Stiles MBE

Chris Moon MBE *was captured in Cambodia by the Khmer Rouge and is one of the few westerners to have survived. He was then blown up by a landmine and lost an arm and a leg. Less than a year after leaving hospital, he ran the London Marathon. He has since ran 250 km across the Sahara, five back-to-back marathons across Death Valley (twice!) and climbed Mount Kilimanjaro.*

Why bother? It's always easier to do nothing.

I can't be bothered, I can't be arsed, it's too much effort, I don't read, I'm just biding my time, so why should I read this book?

This is a great book and the reason this book should be read is because it's an injection of positive energy – pure, prime nutrition for the brain. It'll be good for you . . . You can do more than you think . . . Broaden your horizons.

I've had the good fortune to visit some unusual places, such as countries emerging from civil war, and I was working to clear the debris of war – landmines and unexploded ordnance – in Mozambique, East Africa, when I was blown up losing two limbs. I mention this because it has taught me a great deal.

First, I believe we have so much we take for granted. You shouldn't have to lose something to appreciate its value. Things are changing fast in the modern world. We need to cope with change and recognize we may not be able to stay in the same place if the world is moving on around us. So I had to learn to manage the change and I did this by being open-minded and being prepared to see things from a different perspective.

That's why I believe this book is important. It's all about doing and living life, rather than sitting there and letting life do it to you. In the modern corporate world I find it refreshing that Damian Hughes has written this book, which is a bit like a road atlas for life, so well done for reading it and remember you can do more than you think . . . Everyone can go one step beyond their limits.

Chris Moon MBE

Sir John Jones KBE *has been a head teacher of three secondary schools over a period of 17 years, including the worst-performing school in the UK. He was successful in turning around their performance and was awarded a knighthood for his services to education in 2003.*

The world is full of heroes and our lives are enriched with stories of heroism and heroic deeds.

We all need our legends. However, true heroism is not confined to such places as battlefields or sports arenas. It is found mostly in the day-to-day deeds of ordinary people performing them extraordinarily well. This book gives tribute to such people.

Look around you at home, in the community, on the shop floor, in the workshop and in the office – they are there, showing courage, passion, resilience and the will never to give up, whatever the challenge.

This book will probably surprise you, definitely move you, but mostly inspire you. Perhaps in reading it you will find the courage to be heroic in your own life.

163

Read it, enjoy it and be inspired!

Sir John Jones

Daley Thompson claims more decathlon honours than anyone before or after him. He was the first person to hold World, Olympic, Commonwealth and European Championship titles in the same year as well as a world record. Daley was unbeaten in nine years and was the Olympic Champion in 1980 and 1984, World Champion in 1983, European Champion in 1982 and 1986, and Commonwealth Champion in 1978, 1982 and 1986. He held four world records in his career. Daley was awarded a CBE in 2000 and was voted BBC Sports Personality of the Year in 1982.

As a double Olympic decathlon champion, I am fully aware of the demands that are required to be the best and achieve your dreams. I am very familiar with the tips, skills and techniques demonstrated and I recommend that you take some time and sit and read this book. The skills taught can be invaluable and if applied could change your life!

Daley Thompson

Australian sporting legend Wayne Bennett was an international rugby league footballer in the 1970s and has been the coach of the Brisbane Broncos since 1988. Before that, he was co-coach of the Canberra Raiders. He has won five Premiership titles and had outstanding success at State of Origin level, leading Queensland to victory on four occasions. He is also Australia's national team coach. He is the author of the bestselling book Don't Die with the Music in You.

There are two quotes I use a lot and I think they neatly summarize the content of this book.

" If it's to be, it's up to me. "

and

" People don't fail in life, they just give up trying. "

Use this book to teach yourself never to accept your second best.

Wayne Bennett